We're All White, Thanks:
the persisting myth about 'white' schools

We're All White, Thanks:
the persisting myth about 'white' schools

Chris Gaine

2005

Trentham Print Design

Stoke on Trent, UK and Sterling, USA

Staffordshire

Trentham Books Limited
Westview House   22883 Quicksilver Drive
734 London Road   Sterling
Oakhill   VA 20166-2012
Stoke on Trent   USA
Staffordshire
England ST4 5NP

First published 2005

British Library Cataloguing-in-Publication Data
A catalogue record for this book is available from the British Library

ISBN-13: 978-1-85856-345-9
ISBN-10: 1-85856-345-3

Cover image by Kaï Nadine Costa

Designed and typeset by Trentham Print Design Ltd, Chester and
printed in Great Britain by Cromwell Press Ltd, Trowbridge.

Contents

Preface • vii

Chapter 1
No minorities- no problem • 1

Chapter 2
How did we get here? • 29

Chapter 3
Cycles of productive change • 45

Chapter 4
Words, Concepts, Definitions, Terminology • 69

Chapter 5
Racial incidents in white schools • 101

Chapter 6
What to do: Resources • 125

Chapter 7
Antiracist work in mainly white higher education • 153

Chapter 8
Octopus and Axe, some final notes • 171

References • 181

Index • 187

Preface

This is the third book in a series. *No Problem Here* was published in 1987, having been written in the midst of my involvement over the previous four years with anti-racism in a mainly white secondary school, two teacher training establishments, and an LEA. Having largely completed the manuscript by 1985, I went through some despondent times while publishers pointed out to me that the work was caught in its own trap: if people did not see race as an issue in white schools, no-one would buy the book. They had a point, but the courage of Mark Cohen at Hutchinson paid off and the book, evidently the first to explore the issue, sold very well.

Its sequel – *Still No Problem Here* – was far easier to get published, Gillian Klein at Trentham having become established as an effective supporter of writers on equality issues. But it was harder to write, partly because I was further removed from the heat of daily classroom engagement and nightly curriculum innovation, but also because the political climate had changed from indifference and some curiosity in the 1980s to outright opposition in the 1990s. A long chapter in the 1995 book explores the media and political discourse of the late 1980s and early 1990s that attacked and undermined race equality in schools.

The climate has changed again, and I'm aware there is now a ready audience for this book, that it is again considered legitimate to ask certain questions. I hope the book addresses some of them effectively. It has some different aims from the first two, but essentially seeks to set out the arguments for consistently addressing race equality in schools where some may still think the small numbers of black and minority ethnic pupils do not warrant the effort.

I owe thanks to the many inspiring people I have had the good fortune to work with over my years in this field – too many to list – and to Gillian Klein for encouraging me to write the book and for her editing. Thanks also to the University of Chichester for providing a supportive environment for my work for twenty years.

Chichester
June 2005

1

No minorities – no problem

Recognising the issue

Anyone who has read my previous books will know that I became interested in this work while working as a humanities teacher in a Wiltshire comprehensive in the 1970s. It was the vocabulary of some otherwise very pleasant and amenable young people that first alerted me: they would refer to people as 'niggers' and 'pakis' with no apparent awareness of how offensive it was. On digging a little deeper (but not much) I revealed a web of half truths, misunderstandings, myths and prejudices about 'race' (a contested term) that was alarming because it was so taken for granted, so widely shared, and either so unproblematic or so unnoticed by most of my colleagues.

It was not seen as problematic, even when exposed, because the issue of racism was fundamentally seen as located where there were 'other races' and these were most often distinguished by colour. Although my colleagues and neighbours would not have articulated it this way, the dominant perception was that 'other races' actually caused racism by their presence, that the real issues were to do with first hand conflict over employment, housing and culture. By this logic, there was inevitably more racism when there were more of 'them', so no-one was looking for the disease when the causes of the contagion were at a safe distance. There may be unpalatable things *said*, but really there was 'no problem'.

The flaw in this logic is that racism is in people's heads. Certainly it may have a relationship to material factors like housing but it need not be limited by geography: it travels easily. What I uncovered was that young people with almost no contact with real minority ethnic people *believed* they knew a great deal about them: they knew they 'took our jobs', they 'caused overcrowding', they 'didn't accept our ways' and they 'caused trouble'. Two quotations from my pupils at that time illustrate the point:

> Many people are against coloureds and also against blacks. There is a lot of people who would like to see coloureds and blacks chucked out of this country. They always stir up too much trouble and then don't like being punished for it. Every coloured person wants everyone to give them what they want when they want it. The Pakistanis always wear turbans. The reasons for this is their religion. The Pakis have very strong religion. Most of them are friendly but you get the odd few that are violent. They also do not get married normally because marriages are all arranged. Also they are pigs.

> Black and coloured people are equal to white and any other colour. It doesn't matter what colour you are so long as you are a good kind person. I'm glad Britain accepts any person(s) that are any colour. I am certainly not prejudiced and love the fact that the colour of the skin has nothing to do with the heart. Although we do get thrown back when the question is asked about a black man or lady wanting to marry a white man or lady. Will God accept this? My views on black and coloured people are perfectly normal. Love is the greatest thing since Moses parted the sea. Also comparing the church [Christian] with the black church [gospel] I prefer the gospel church. Any colour does not matter, it's your personality that counts. Pakistanis are the same as anybody although they don't tend to be social with anyone else they stick to their own language, so I think if they're gonna be like that they can go back to their own country. I don't mind the colour but when it comes to the religion I will rule that out, all this babble and boys having to grow long hair, heads in turbans and hankies. What a load of rubbish. (Gaine, 1987: 7-8)

I found such sentiments expressed in white areas in various parts of Britain, leading me to argue that this was not simple ignorance. Their views were not random collections of muddled ideas, they were patterned: the same stereotyped, negative, detailed myths were recited all the way from Cumbria to Cornwall. I called it 'learned misinformation', and the task facing schools was not that they were facing a blank slate. They did not have young people who believed they knew nothing about minorities, but young people who believed they knew a lot, and what they 'knew' was negative.

I will consider later in this chapter to what extent these kinds of views can still be found, but that aside, much has happened since. At times the issue I identified then has been recognised as one education should tackle; at others it has been relegated to something marginal and peripheral, or worse still as only the concern of hopeless idealists and malcontents who don't appreciate that the pursuit of measurable 'standards' will solve all educational ills. I discuss this a little in Chapter 2.

In the meantime, what of the society our children are now growing up into? The phrase 'Britain is a multicultural society' is quite widely used nowadays, to the annoyance of those who regret the fact and to the confusion of some others. It's partly true and it partly isn't.

Social and demographic changes

What is usually being referred to in the phrase multicultural society is the arrival since the late 1940s of numbers of people from former colonial possessions: the Indian sub-continent, the Caribbean, Hong Kong, and Africa: not to put too fine a point on it, black, brown and Chinese people. In one sense we have all got used to *visibility*. We are pretty familiar with black and Asian faces on TV screens, in pop music, in football teams, in a few high profile positions in public life. We are also used to the multiculturalising of food, with ubiquitous Chinese and Indian restaurants, Thai food hot in pursuit, and all the supermarket chains selling 'ethnic' ingredients and ready meals.

More recently, in addition to this *Empire Strikes Back* meaning about 'visible' minorities, multicultural might also be taken to include people from the EU, a belated recognition of many from pre-EU Eire, from Eastern Europe, refugees from around the world and a greater emphasis on religious difference. Going further, it might recognise the historic diversity represented by Scotland, Wales and Northern Ireland, and the presence of Jews and Travellers.

But *really*, when people say multicultural how much do they still mean 'colour'? Does the term 'ethnic ingredients' bring to mind pasta as much as popadoms? How much of race remains an issue of visibility? My brief answer to these questions is that visibility continues to fix race in people's minds, and that in practice ethnicity is often 'coloured' too. I am going to argue in this book that while new subtleties and complexities have arisen (or were always there but have been belatedly understood), colour remains a critical, distorting and dangerous signifier of difference and inequality, and that this is truer of white areas than more ethnically mixed ones.

Some context: numbers

Despite the frequently repeated mantra that Britain is multicultural, in two senses it is not as multicultural as all that: neither in terms of actual numbers nor in terms of dispersal and distribution. Since so much of this debate is accompanied by a kind of muzak of mythology about the facts of diversity, I shall set out the best data we have. The 2001 Census showed that everyone who did *not* describe themselves as white British amounted to 12.5 per cent of the population. Some of these are *white but not British*, having roots for instance in other parts of Europe, or Canada, New Zealand and Australia. Others are *British but not white*: 8 per cent have a heritage in parts of the non-white Commonwealth but almost half of these are British born. About 10 per cent of the population overall were born outside the UK. It's worth reading these figures again, since they don't correspond with each other. British born doesn't mean white, white doesn't mean British, black doesn't mean non-British.

Using the specific groupings employed in the Census, we can say this about the most commonly used ethnic distinctions within the UK population:

ETHNIC GROUPS IN THE UK, %	
White	92.1
Mixed	1.2
Indian	1.8
Pakistani	1.3
Bangladeshi	0.5
Other Asian	0.4
Black Caribbean	1.0
Black African	0.8
Other Black	0.2
Chinese	0.4
Other ethnic groups	0.4

Source: ONS, 2001 Census

And to signal early on that religion is an increasingly important signifier of difference, the Census data are telling. More than 70 per cent described themselves as Christian (not all of them white, of course). About one and a half million follow Islam (2.7 per cent), a little over half a million are Hindu, 330,000 are Sikh and 266,000 are Jewish, with Buddhists making up the next largest group at 150,000, or 0.3 per cent (Richardson, 2004a: 28).

Overall figures are misleading, however, since while 9 per cent of the population are from visible ethnic minorities this percentage is not evenly spread. No one from Cornwall or Northumberland or Norfolk encounters this proportion in the local population, neither in fact do residents of some counties adjoining the big cities. The reality is that Britain's multicultural element is mainly to be found in London and the industrial cites. Nationally 0.5 per cent of the population are of Bangladeshi descent, but in Tower Hamlets this reaches 33 per cent. Nationally one per cent of the population is African-Caribbean, but they comprise 10 per cent of Lambeth's population. There are 160 Indians in Herefordshire, but they make up a quarter of Leicester's population. In one town just north of London, one in nine of the population is Jewish. Overall, 45 per cent of black and minority ethnic people live in the greater London region (ONS, 2005). Since we are primarily concerned with education, it is also worth noting that overall numbers mask different age structures, with the young making up higher proportions of most (not all) minority ethnic groups.

PERCENTAGE AGE DISTRIBUTION: BY ETHNIC GROUP, 2001/02

	Under 16	16-64	65 and over	All ages
White	19	65	16	92.1
Mixed	55	43	2	1.2
Indian	22	71	6	1.8
Pakistani	35	61	4	1.3
Bangladeshi	38	58	3	0.5
Other Asian	22	74	4	0.4
Black Caribbean	25	67	9	1.0
Black African	33	66	2	0.8
Other Black	35	60	5	0.2
Chinese	18	77	5	0.4
Other ethnic groups	20	76	4	0.4

Source, ONS, 2001 Census

The outcome of this variable pattern of settlement for schools is that while there is scarcely a secondary school in the land without some minority ethnic pupils (there are only eight small LEAs that have very few or no schools with more than 4 per cent) in about two thirds of them they make up less than 5 percent, and 25 per cent of primary schools really are 'all white' (DfES, 2003).

A very diverse diversity

To develop this further, whereas we might use the shorthand 'white areas' or 'white schools' to refer to the areas where there is little visible diversity, we might usefully refine this into considering that there are broadly three types of such areas: adjacent – certain areas within multi-ethnic cities; peripheral – commuter belts close to multi-ethnic cities; and isolated.

Adjacent areas are those whose populations inhabit a largely white area but are part of a multi-ethnic city in most aspects of their lives. There are some such areas in London, though these are never far from the other characteristic of London already noted: the country's highest residential concentrations of black and Asian people. Similar contrasts adjacent to each other can be found in Birmingham, Manchester, Bradford and other British industrial cities. This parallel existence of very white areas alongside much more mixed ones usually, but not always, includes schooling. There are some white primary schools in very mixed areas because of social class: either local housing costs are very high and therefore excluding, or an established public housing estate might remain almost as white as it was in the 1950s. Minorities in such areas usually have ready access to religious and cultural contact elsewhere in the city.

There are also areas *peripheral* to these cities, like parts of the rural Midlands, which in addition, make considerable use of the city by commuting into it for work, shopping and entertainment. Here there is more separation between the 'whiteness' of people's residential, social and school lives and their contact with black and Asian people in other spheres. Minorities here will have some access to others in their community, though they will generally have to travel.

Broadly speaking, there is a third level of separateness: *isolation* – exemplified most obviously by Norfolk or Cornwall, north Wales and all of rural Scotland – where most of the population have virtually no first hand contact with Asian and black people at all, in any aspect of life. The eight small LEAs referred to above are in this category. The term 'isolated' also applies to any minorities that live there: practising faith communities or those sharing a language may be too far away for regular contact, and local public services will have little experience if and when their support is needed. In such areas it can be misleading to refer to 'communities' or 'the minority ethnic community' because there probably isn't one. To underline this, in some unpublished research for a rural county (Gaine, 2005) I was surprised at the proportion of the minority ethnic population who were (in terms of Census categories) 'mixed', including 'Asian mixed', who are not a common group nationally. Cline *et al* (2002) found something similar.

The levels are far more complicated than mere geography. Depending on occupation, social class, gender, family connections and age, some people in outer London will be to all intents and purposes 'isolated' while others in Hampshire could almost be in the 'adjacent' category. Young people in the shires, especially those at school, are likely to be more isolated from black and Asian people than parents who commute; young people schooled in 'adjacent' areas are likely to have more contact with black and Asian people than many of their parents, for whom occupation and long-established social networks might maintain separation (Gaine, 2000: 66-7).

More context: media, politics and public attitudes
The good news
In Chapter 2 I suggest that the political and educational climate we now live and work in is significantly more positive about combating racial inequality than was the case when I was writing *Still No Problem Here* in the mid 1990s. There are (some) voices within the Labour Party that speak of the issue with courage and conviction rather than a wary eye on white votes; certain influences from the EU have had a positive effect (like legislating against religious discrimination) and most significantly of all the Race Relations Amendment Act has had a legitimising effect that I will discuss in more detail later. There is a continuing pressure to monitor race and its effects consistently and thoroughly. Travellers have been given a higher profile as a group whose educational needs have to be recognised (e.g. DfES, 2003).

The bad news

Not everything the government has done or said is positive. Some of it is contradictory, some utterances by significant figures either pro-vocative or ill-informed or both – a Home Secretary on 'swamping'; a Chief Inspector on Muslim schooling; a Prime Minister on refugees. The mass media, especially television, both reinforce and diminish the effects of living in a mainly white area (Downing and Husband, 2005). On the one hand they bring a multicultural society into every-one's living room, probably contributing to the myth that a huge pro-portion of the country's population is black and Asian. With depress-ing echoes of what young people said to me 20 years ago, in 2004 a MORI survey found a widespread perception that 25 per cent of the population were 'immigrants'. On the other hand, media representa-tions can keep racial difference at a distance, potentially exotic, puzz-ling, or threatening (van Dijk: 1987, 1993; Downing and Husband, 2005). Over a decade ago, Troyna and Hatcher (1992) highlighted the contradictory nature of such media influence, arguing in their study of primary school children in mainly white schools that positive anti-racist messages, usually from soaps, are recognised and cited by chil-dren, along with messages about stereotyped Africans and all black people's alleged genetic predisposition to violence and sporting prowess.

Some issues can move up the agenda. In 2004 MORI found what they described as a 'monumental shift in people's concerns' on national issues, immigration coming third behind education and health. What is meant by immigration has also changed. Whereas in the 1990s the race issue in the media, politics and public attitudes mainly referred to those from former colonial territories, more re-cently asylum seekers of any colour or origin have become among the targets:

> Of the 45% who believe the welfare state treats them as second-class citizens, 39% blame asylum seekers and new immigrants. Surveys 10 years ago showed anxiety about 'freeloading' by lone parents and the unemployed, but now asylum seekers are the focus of resent-ment. (*Guardian*, 2004)

Some issues do not change as much as we might hope. After 30 years of increasingly draconian immigration laws it is still possible for politicians to describe the UK as a soft touch, as having a shambolic immigration service, so inevitably on the point of being overwhelmed by 'foreign scroungers'. A poll commissioned by the BBC in 2002 asked whether immigration had damaged or benefited Britain in the past 50 years. Forty seven per cent of white people thought it had had a damaging effect; related questions showing 69 per cent thought people didn't integrate or have a positive effect (BBC, 2002). The same poll found an acknowledgment by 52 per cent of white people that 'Britain is a racist society'. Commenting on his own poll, MORI's research director said 'We have overestimated the progress we have made in race and immigration issues'.

It is too simplistic to blame the media: the interplay between the media and politicians and their joint construction of news are what generates new race agendas and concerns. These now have three added dimensions: refugees, white migrant workers, and Muslims.

On the first two, big numbers are not involved. The statistics given earlier still characterise the largest multicultural element in Britain, but refugees, migrant workers and terrorist Muslims have caught the imagination of the public, not without help from the media and the politicians.

Refugees

I can't unravel all this here, this is not that kind of book. But it is worth stressing that per head of population the UK has ranked 8th in Europe and 19th in the world for taking in refugees over the past decade (UNHCR, 2004), that Germany has taken in significantly more, and that everyone pales into significance beside the two countries that have taken in two million apiece: Pakistan and Iran. The media consistently flout their own guidelines in using legally meaningless terms such as 'illegal asylum seekers' (*Guardian*, 2004). Small wonder that the public overestimate by ten times the number of refugees claiming asylum in the UK, believe that most of the world's refugees come here, and strongly associate the term 'illegal immigrant' with media reporting of the issues (MORI, 2002). The same survey found that young people were also less informed of refugee issues and therefore less likely to have a positive impression than the overall population.

As for *foreign workers*, Britain attracts them because it has a labour shortage. This was of particular relevance in the general election year of 2005, when all politicians knew that the main source of immigration had shifted to Eastern Europe, with close to 100,000 young workers entering the country in the previous year or so to take up the many low paid service sector and farming jobs employers were desperate to fill. Despite this, there was campaigning against immigration using the word immigration as a code word for colour and cultural difference, preferring to use this code with the electorate rather than explain what was really happening. Indeed, the Conservatives kept repeating that they were not racist to raise the issue of immigration. Neither their manifesto nor any of their leaders ever stated that most immigration was white, yet to do so would surely have been their most obvious defence against criticism of this kind.

Little has been done to clarify the confusion in many people's minds between these Eastern European workers and, say, Kosovan refugees. Failing to point out how many of these workers work in health and social care, while simultaneously expressing concern about the 'strain on public services caused by immigration' does nothing to foster a genuine public debate and contributes to the 'learned misinformation' that schools then have to unravel.

Not all migrant workers are from Eastern Europe, but it is ironic that a significant proportion of recent immigrants who are not white have been specifically recruited, mainly from Africa, to work as nurses. These numbered 13,000 in 2004, but the media and political defining of the issue means a black nurse on her way to work is likely to be perceived as a refugee or an illegal immigrant. In the last two weeks of the 2005 election campaign, when 'immigration' as an issue was receiving maximum publicity, a black woman I know was awoken from a snooze in a park by thirteen year olds throwing stones at her. She wasn't the only person taking advantage of the warm weather, but she was the only black one, and it had never happened to her before.

The end result is that hostility to these new arrivals – whether workers or refugees, whether from Europe or Africa – is couched in terms of threat, scarce resources, and being the undeserving poor. It is as if there is a series of buttons that can easily be pressed, a series of responses readily invoked with the right collection of symbolic prompts: Britishness, scroungers, bogus, foreign ways, inexplicit threats.

Islam

The notion of a threat takes us to one of the common perceptions of Muslims: that they present a terrorist threat, one that overlaps with another common perception that Muslims are all inflexible fundamentalists and hence a threat to British culture. As the Runnymede Trust (1997) showed, this is not new. Neither is it simply a product of 9/11; it has its roots long ago and was fuelled by the Rushdie affair in the late 1980s. Nevertheless, it has found new momentum. There was evidence of a rise and fall in anti-Islamic sentiment after the event itself (Gaine and Lamley, 2003; Sheridan, 2002), expressed in relation to terrorism but also in terms of Muslims being too 'traditional' and 'unBritish', as well as being oppressive to women – not that this prevented some women recognisable by their head covering being targeted for abuse. Different potential views of Islam are well summarised in the following table.

Closed, prejudiced view of Islam, seen as ..	Open, unprejudiced view of Islam, seen as ..
The same everywhere, unchanging, unbending	Varying in different places, with Muslims debating changes and different views
Having no ideas and values in common with other faiths, and no links with them	Having some shared ideas and aims and valuing communication
Inferior to Europe and the USA, barbaric, primitive, sexist	Different but not inferior, and worthy of respect
Violent, aggressive, threatening	Peaceful and maybe a partner in co-operating and solving shared problems
Not European	Having a long history within Europe with an influence in science and architecture
Not belonging in Britain	The faith of many British, French and German people, so is here to stay
Always unfairly critical of 'the West'	Perhaps having a view on life and the world worth listening to
Too strict, especially on girls and young people	Having strong moral standards
Seen only as political ideology	Seen as genuine and sincerely practised religious faith
Anti-Muslim hostility seen as natural and 'normal'	Critical views of Islam themselves subject to critique

Derived from Runnymede Trust, (1997: 5)

Certainly the 9/11 bombings in the USA and those in London in July 2005 *were* carried out by Muslims, but the notion that all Muslims constitute a threat of one kind or another is simplistic, oppressive and wrong. It is summarised by the left hand column and countered on the right.

The research cited above by both Gaine and Lamley (2003) and Sheridan (2002) demonstrate that the hostility being expressed is cultural and not 'racial' in the old biological sense. The British National Party have latched onto this in their campaigning and avoid the restrictions of the Race Relations Act by inciting hostility to Muslims, pretty much along the lines of the left hand column above, rather than a group strictly definable by colour. This is one of the several reasons for the 2005 proposal to introduce a law against the incitement to religious hatred.

On the other hand, my observations above and in Chapter 3 about hostility still often being rooted in colour or race are borne out by a *Telegraph* columnist who wrote

> Orientals ... shrink from pitched battle, which they often deride as a sort of game, preferring ambush, surprise, treachery and deceit as the best way to overcome an enemy.... This war [in Afghanistan] belongs within the much larger spectrum of a far wider conflict between settled, creative, productive Westerners and predatory, destructive Orientals. (Keegan, *Daily Telegraph*, 8 October 2001)

Quite apart from the sweeping offensiveness of what he is saying, there seems to me to be a dangerous slippage here between a cultural accusation and an apparent inherent, inbuilt disposition of 'Orientals'.

What is less often reported about Muslims is their relative disadvantage compared to other 'Asians' and to whites. This is relatively easy to track since virtually all British Pakistanis and Bangladeshis are Muslim, and we know, for instance that

- Bangladeshis and Pakistanis are two and a half times more likely to be unemployed than the white population and three times more likely to be on low pay

- three-quarters of Bangladeshi and Pakistani children live in households earning less than half the average income

- 54 per cent of Pakistani and Bangladeshi homes receive income support, three times other households

- 28 per cent of older Pakistani and Bangladeshi people live in homes without central heating

- Perinatal mortality rate among Pakistani mothers is 16 per cent, twice the UK average

- 20 per cent of Muslims report a long-standing illness, compared with 16 per cent for Hindus and Sikhs. (derived from Home Office, 2005: 16-23; *Guardian* June 17, 2002)

If there is disenchantment and alienation among British Muslims, we might profitably look at their experience in Britain rather than invoke international conspiracies or a genetic predisposition to treachery.

Minority experience in white areas

So much for the national context. I argue in this book that the main reason for promoting race equality in schools in majority white areas is that the majority need it. They need it partly for their futures in a Britain that will never again be the white society of myth and memory, but they also need it to be informed young citizens.

> [In Dorset] an Indian commented that people frequently (wrongly) assumed he was either a doctor or a shopkeeper; a teenager of mixed heritage said local villagers seemed at first to regard him as a potential gangster; others were tired of the assumption they would be good dancers, footballers or athletes... (Gaine and Lamley, 2003: 44)

Thus, to emphasise the educational case we should pay attention to the experience and perceptions of black and minority ethnic people where they live, work and go to school in small numbers. Much of the research and the national data about racial discrimination in various aspects of life refer to urban areas. This is inevitable since it is where most of the targets of discrimination are. There are, however, a number of studies about rural racism from which it can be seen that, while experience is complex and varied and not easily reducible to generalisations, the idea of 'no problem here' certainly does not apply to life in and out of school (Carroll, 2003; Collins and Begum, 2002; Connolly and Keenan, 2000; DEED, 1998; de Lima, 2001; Dhalech, 1999 and 2000; Donald *et al*, 1995; Gaine and Lamley, 2003; Gough and Gaine, 2002; Henderson and Kaur, 1999; Jay, 1992; Kenny,

1997; NCVO, 1994; Norfolk REC, 1994). In the most recent and largest of these, based upon 200 interviews, conducted in an area that was mainly 'isolated' with a 'peripheral' urban area, one young black parent observed:

> ... being a Black person living in a predominantly white area is not fun because you are always seen as different and as having less status/importance than others. Some of the neighbours bring in old furniture or toys without asking whether we need them because they think that we are not as wealthy as them. ... I think that it is due to the ideas that they already have on Black people, that they are normally poor, and less wealthy. My kids are sometimes called names because of their skin colour and bullied. ... No matter how hard we try to immerse in the society, we are always regarded as outsiders or as less human than white people. (Gaine and Lamley, 2003: 44)

There are some clear patterns and some variations. The school students we interviewed were rarely ground down or crushed by the negative experiences they had had, and neither were many of the adults. Indeed, some people in all our studies and from a range of backgrounds have always felt positively welcomed in the area in which they live. The majority had means and strategies to deal with racist experiences. Some challenged, some retaliated, some ignored, some 'forgave' and 'rose above it'. While some people felt strong enough in themselves to 'cope with crass, ill-formed or racist comments and actions', most acknowledged it 'had some effect' and a minority found overt hostility undermining and damaging, but for some uncertainty had become a pervading sense of threat.

Many informants felt varying degrees of marginalisation and exclusion, from subtle signals, to humiliating treatment at shop checkouts, to suspicion, to barriers in seeking help from local agencies, to perhaps not gaining employment, to racist insults, to actual violence. Name-calling was relatively common, most often from strangers, and in this and physical harassment the perpetrators were most often young men.

Such experiences varied greatly, and while there are no simple explanations for this we did find that there was less variation in experiences within the same ethnic group and that a high income or a good job did not necessarily afford protection. Visibility because of skin colour was often a key factor in explicit exclusion, as was being identified – or misidentified – as a Muslim. Minorities seem to be expected to tolerate 'jokes' about their ethnicity. Some did, but even European white people without such a history of being stigmatised found the repetition of these 'jokes' and common assumptions about them tedious and sometimes painful. People from visible minorities were unambiguous about such 'jokes' being racist and offensive. Some black people report a kind of innocent naivety, curiosity ('can I touch your hair?') and anxiety about colour and its terminology not found in more cosmopolitan areas of Britain. Black respondents often felt subject to negative and patronising stereotypes and out-dated ideas.

In a series of interviews and focus groups in one of the studies re-ferred to above we found that within twenty minutes a group of minority ethnic young people[1] could produce this catalogue of ex-periences:

What's happened to you personally?
    Name-calling: 'Paki', 'Chinko', 'Jap', 'Arab', 'nigger'
    Told 'Go back to your own country'
    Overheard racist jokes
    Neighbouring school's pupils racially abusive
    Accent and name mocked
    Looked at in a different way from white friends in public places
    People act differently, mistrustful
    Customer refused to be served by me at Saturday job
    Sister asked if related to Osama Bin Laden
    Muslim neighbour and myself had insulting notes left on doorsteps
    Racist threatening text messages and phone-calls
    Spat at from a passing bus
    Serious verbal fights over race
    Physical fight over race

What's happened to your home and family?
    Racist words scratched into car paint
    House attacked
    Father insulted in his car
    Car kicked
    Stones thrown, eggs throw
    Physical racist attacks on adult family members
    Moved house because of harassment
    Aware of racial discrimination experienced by parents
    Patient refusing medical treatment from [Asian] parent

Encouraged by parents to work twice as hard to get anywhere
Aware of graffiti and attacks on minority university students
Some belief that the authorities don't really do anything about
racism

Are there more subtle things that happen that get you down?
People have negative assumptions about us speaking another
language
People speak slowly to me in English
Assumptions about me being slow and poor
I get stared at
Unconscious racism, people don't know what they're saying
sometimes
'The darker the skin the worse it is'
If you're light skinned, then some assume you will agree with
racism!
You still get trouble even if very westernised
If you complain 'you're just moaning', if you stay silent it goes
unchecked.
(Gaine and Lamley, 2003: 34)

As I intimated earlier, the striking thing about these young people
was that they were not hapless victims: they were confident, mostly
academically successful and generally optimistic. They regarded
racism as an extra struggle they had to contend with, but like most of
their parents they planned to succeed despite it. They had all heard
the message that they would have to work considerably harder than
a white person of the same ability to be recognised. One might therefore say 'so what, they are coping' but I would argue that they should
not have to, that this is a set of barriers a genuinely multicultural
society should want to get out of their way.

We summarised the broader issues they and their families faced as:
being marginal, being marginalised, and being targeted, and we
characterised a common dilemma as being between belonging and
being separate. This resonates with Cline *et al*'s findings:

Some parents reported that their children had begun to resist their
attempts to acculturate them into their home culture. They offered
examples of children who resisted learning their home language or
wanted to keep cultural traditions (e.g. over types of food) hidden
from their white friends. Most of the parents were prepared to accept
this behaviour, associating it with their child's need to act 'English' or

'British' when at school. But, when they justified this in terms of the child avoiding 'embarrassment', they begged an uncomfortable question – should attending a mainly white school necessarily lead to a sense of embarrassment about distinctive aspects of a minority ethnic heritage? (2002: 150)

In their lives they have to negotiate the issues summed up in some of their own phrases, their complicity in racism being assumed if they are light skinned; the 'promise' that if they assimilate prejudice will disappear; the pressure to 'take a joke', and the assumption that only trouble makers or those with chips on their shoulders complain and the uncertainty about whether they are being treated differently as a person or as part of a racial or ethnic group.

When informed of findings like these the CEO of a another shire county said, in a speech to a county conference:

I didn't realise that these issues were of such serious importance in the kind of area in which we live and work, or that these children were being subjected to this kind of racist experience as young citizens. (cited in Carroll, 2003: 151)

School perspectives

All this raises a particular problem for schools. When there are no or very few minority ethnic children in the class compared with when they make up 50 per cent or more, the agenda is very different in the playground, in classroom dynamics, in parents' consciousness and in teachers' priorities. This is inevitable and it would be naive to expect otherwise. Still, the context of legal requirements, media representation, political positioning and public attitudes means race is on the agenda. In a national system of education schools have several roles. However one interprets it, there is a role to prepare for adult life. Government enjoins schools to respond positively to the multicultural nature of British society, indeed it goes further, expecting them to take a proactive role in working against racism (Home Office, 2000). Nevertheless, in the fourteen schools they researched in four different regions of the country, Cline *et al* found:

In six of our fourteen schools no teacher we spoke to mentioned multicultural education or any related theme in connection with that age range. No school in this sample had a fully developed strategy for preparing pupils through the curriculum for life in a diverse society. (2002: 94)

These findings can be distilled into three overlapping motives for engaging with the issue of race equality, whatever the makeup of the school:

■ *Pragmatic motive*: the law and Ofsted require it. It is no longer negotiable or optional. For a school to avoid the risk of legal non-compliance or negative Ofsted feedback it has to consider what it does with regard to race and racism.

■ *Principled motive (a)*: equipping majority young people with an education appropriate for a society where they may live next to, become related to by marriage or relationships, work with, manage or be managed by black and minority ethnic people. This entails affirming people's rights to fair treatment and understanding that diversity is not necessarily to be feared.

■ *Principled motive (b)*: providing a safe and affirming educational experience for minority pupils.

The first of these is addressed in more practical detail in Chapter 3. Here I consider the principled motives.

Principled motive (a): young majority attitudes

In *Still No Problem Here* (1995) I described four simple exercises to take the racist temperature in white areas of our society, each one targeting a different age group. The first is designed for young children and was first described by Jeffcoate in 1979. One simply invites a class of young children to imagine they are in a hot air balloon which can take them anywhere they want to go, and the task is for them to draw and write about wherever that is. However on the way home the balloon is blown off course to a country they really, really don't want to go to, maybe far away. They have to say where it is and what happens to them there. The results highlight the images and ideas already in such young minds about which places are to be avoided and why. These places tended then to be populated by dark skinned people with guns or spears.

The next litmus test is designed for ten year olds and is quite similar: they are sitting at home one day, there is a knock at the door, and when they open it they find standing there a black man, or someone Chinese or Indian. A control group open the door to a taxi driver. They then write a story about what happens next. I gave some examples then which I can summarise as: almost 60 per cent showed some sense of anxiety, fear, threat or pity when a visible minority character faced them on their doorstep.

With slightly older pupils, say 14 year olds, the task is to write a couple of paragraphs about some current affairs topics. Anything in the news will do, but in 2005 I would suggest: the royal family; binge drinking; dieting and obesity, and immigration – asylum seekers and terrorism produce material with a 'racial' element, too. The point of choosing four topics in that order is so they do not realise you are really after their views on race. It should come as no surprise when the exercise reveals comments like 'asylum seekers should leave forever' and a widespread idea that minority ethnic people are given special treatment in getting jobs.

The final exercise is the simplest of all, and I use it on young adults, typically university students. Each is given an index card and asked to write on it simply 'What have you heard about black people and Asian people? What do people say?' This produces dramatic but simple results: what they have heard is overwhelmingly negative. This is particularly interesting in an institution like my own where most of the students have grown up in mainly white areas. What they have heard is not first hand experience, neither is it based upon the first hand experience of those they heard it from. Where the student group are trainee teachers, the collated cards make the case powerfully that the education they provide to future pupils might serve them better than their own schooling did.

Whatever age phase a reader works in, I would suggest trying one of these strategies. It may even encourage reading this book beyond this chapter!

On the whole I do not believe the negative ideas and hostile stereotypes held by many young people necessarily manifest themselves in harassment and deliberately hostile treatment. In so far as they do, this is discussed in Chapter 5. But a fellow pupil may have highly stereotyped and demeaning ideas about Africans as a whole but still have a close friend with African roots. Children (and adults) may simultaneously hold images of frightening Muslims alongside friendship of a Muslim in their class. 'You're all right, but it's all the others' or 'You're like one of us' are some of the mechanisms employed to resolve these contradictions. We should not be fooled, however, by the integration and acceptance of individuals into thinking all is well, and the exercises suggested above will soon reveal that it is not. Chapter 5 also tackles these more embedded aspects of what is best described as cultural racism.

Principled motive (b): young minority experience
It would be untrue to portray life in white schools as some kind of racist hell:

> The majority of the children who had been at their school for a significant length of time were well integrated socially and enjoyed the same range of patterns of friendship within their peer group as would be expected of any other children in these schools. (Cline *et al*, 2002: 6)

But Cline also found they are more likely to feel negatively about their schools because of racist name calling and bullying, and this tended to apply more to younger children

> A significant proportion of the minority ethnic pupils reported race-related name-calling or verbal abuse at school or while travelling to and from school. For example, in the questionnaire survey 26 per cent said that they had had such experiences during the previous week. (*ibid*: 1)

Chapter 5 takes up this aspect of minorities' experiences directly, with strategies for staff to examine and consider school responses, but it also takes up the messages minority pupils receive about their colour and their culture.

To return to the need for an appropriate education, one might ask 'if not now, when?' I have outlined Britain's increasing diversity, and this is going to develop and will never go into reverse. Britain faces both racial/ethnic diversity and inequality related to that diversity, and both these features are slowly spreading. Minorities will grow as a proportion of the population even if there is no further immigration, because a higher proportion of minorities are of childbearing age. Minorities will increasingly move outside the metropolitan areas. Whereas I might characterise the key argument now as being the education of the majority, increasingly it will be minority children in everyone's classroom who will be ill-served if we stay in a rural mind-set.

The paradox of antiracism

A common stumbling block for teachers in white areas is uncertainty about how and when to notice colour and ethnicity. There is certainly an apparent paradox: I argue that race ought not to matter, it ought to be irrelevant, yet I keep drawing attention to it. The message of antiracism is that race – especially in its crudest meaning of colour – should not matter, should not be noticed, yet at the same time it dwells upon it, draws people's attention to it, presses people to notice it.

A common response to this is 'shouldn't we all be colour blind?', to which my answer is, paradoxically, both no and yes. No, at least for the time being, because race matters in people's lives; it is sometimes so relevant so we have to notice it, monitor it, refer to it, examine it, pick at it, in order that we can make it *not* matter. But yes, because people's lives would be better if it were irrelevant, if it did not matter. But that the ideal that colour be irrelevant in social interaction and people's life chances is not the same as society being like that – it isn't. Believing in colour blindness does not of itself make it happen. This was put rather well in the Parekh Report (Runnymede, 2000), which spoke of discriminating *against* and discriminating *between*. We need to discriminate between people in order to make sure we don't discriminate against them. We have to pay attention to race and colour more in order to make them matter less.

So we need to notice race and colour in the majority population's assumptions, not pretend they are not there. We need to understand the different perceptions of minorities, not assume they are indistinguishable from the majority's. We need to know how minorities' experiences of some aspects of life can be different (and worse) in order to try to change the situation. The idea that if we just stop talking about it, writing about it, having laws and policies about it, then everything will be all right is a naïve view of social change. It is also a view that would not be applied to disability rights, for example. I find it hard to imagine someone arguing 'If we stop drawing attention to how disabled people may be treated badly then any unequal treatment will stop'.

That is a shorthand answer to those who say 'don't we all want to be colour blind?' But it is not quite so straightforward, because who is 'we'? Is it a white 'we' that assumes the agreement of people who are perceived as having a colour (as opposed to 'whites' who have none?)

The more complex flaw in the wish for 'colour blindness' is to do with pride in one's colour.

For people who would describe themselves as 'black' their blackness[2] is inevitably a signifier of a history; it is not just a colour. Stuart Hall (1990) calls it a badge. For many individuals it's a badge worn with pride because it signifies survival, their family's and their own survival of centuries of domination in one form or another by Europeans. In that sense what would it mean to be colour blind? It would mean to forget history, to forget how they got here, to forget the survival strategies that helped. So being proud of being black doesn't mean pride in the colour as such, after all its inherent meaning is no more than having freckles.

Being proud of whiteness is not like that. For white people to forget colour entirely entails historical amnesia, as would being unambiguously proud to be white. This is not to say that white British people have nothing to be proud of, but we ought not to be proud of how much the industrial revolution was founded upon the slave trade and exploitative trade with India, how it was buttressed with profits from the opium wars started to addict large sections of the Chinese population and thence protect our tea trade; we ought not to be proud of the atrocities carried out in colonial Kenya to preserve colonial rule (Elkins, 2005); we ought not to be proud of the discrimination that visible minorities have experienced in Britain in the past 50 years; we ought not to be proud of the whiteness involved in the scandal of Stephen Lawrence's murder investigation. We shouldn't be proud of these things and we shouldn't forget them, because part of their legacy is that colour still matters. Colour is what Modood (1992) refers to as 'the mode of oppression' for visible minorities.

Telling someone dark skinned 'I don't notice your colour' is usually meant in a benign way, and may be meant as 'of course I see it but it doesn't obscure you as a person'. However, it is self-deceiving, since their colour would have to have been noticed for the remark to have been made, but secondly it is trying to deny something that is important to them. They may wish it was not, they may wish that like white people they could walk down the street and not potentially be part of a colour, but that is seldom possible, as we have seen. Thirdly, however, such a statement is also a denial of whiteness, a denial of the privilege that whiteness endows, a qualitatively different experience to everyday life. The complexities of this can be illustrated in a partly inverted way by considering the effect of a female infant school Head saying to her first male employee: don't worry, 'I don't see you as man....'

This takes us back to the paradox and a context in which colour blindness as a stance is often invoked: ethnic monitoring. I have little patience with the white people who don't complete monitoring forms on the basis that colour shouldn't matter. In effect they are denying the significance of their own colour, denying that it confers advantage. It does not diminish this advantage to leave the form blank, it obscures it, because without the information employers or educational institutions do not know how many minorities have applied, how many were shortlisted, and so on. Complying assumes on behalf of minorities a liberal state; a state that will not use the information on ethnicity to discriminate more effectively, but for the moment I see no alternative but to make this assumption. Effective monitoring makes any such discriminatory processes transparent and the law makes them actionable. That is the point of having laws and monitoring. The alternative is the pretence of colour blindness and employers simply asserting that they do not discriminate, and there being no means of testing the claim.

Another example relates to dealing with racist incidents and is explored in detail in Chapter 5; I draw attention to the visibility that many minorities experience, the special character of such experience that is obscured by attempting to be colour blind. A recent study in mainly white schools in Bedfordshire, Essex, Norfolk and Suffolk concluded:

> The extent and seriousness of racist incidents was underestimated by teachers and schools. There was a reluctance amongst victims of racial abuse to report incidents for fear of reprisal. Teachers tended to classify racist incidents along with other forms of teasing and bullying, rather than as racist incidents as such, and racist name-calling was not taken seriously enough. (Hamilton *et al*, 1999: 6)

Difficulty, uncertainty and embarrassment about how much to notice race is particularly evident in white areas. Race is present but remote, an issue but not an issue, something really to do with Birmingham, but still, something to vote about. This enhances the paradox because my purpose is to foreground issues of race when it is less present in everyday life, when it is on the edge of white consciousness, where there is a wish not to pay attention to it and yet to be covertly aware of it. It's the elephant in the living room. If you doubt this, consider what will most quickly generate a serious argument at the bar of the *Dog and Duck*.

Part of the understandable confusion in this field, however, is that there ought to be no such paradox with ethnicity. I discuss some uncertainty and fudging of the concept of ethnicity in Chapter 5, but if it involves shared aspects of culture like language, religion, a common history and some sense of identity as a group, how insulting can it be to say 'I don't notice your ethnicity'? The goal or ideal of an ethnic-blind society makes little sense. Ethnicity is not, in Modood's terms (1992: 48), a mode of oppression, it's a 'mode of being'; it's how people choose to be, how they express themselves, an important element in how they construct their identity. It's a cultural term not a biological one; ethnicity is what you do, not what you are. So the paradox about noticing race applies much less to ethnicity: it's highly relevant to people's lives and to how they see themselves and we should not try to be 'ethnic blind'. In summing up their findings on this issue Cline *et al* comment:

> Aspects of ethnicity were central in the pupils' self-identification. The most important features of their ethnic self-characterisation appeared to stem from their families. A sense of ethnic identity was promoted by parents through teaching their children their home language or religious and cultural values and through involving them in contacts with and visits to networks of relatives and friends from the same ethnic background. An additional factor influencing how they saw their ethnic identity was the way in which they and other members of their ethnic group were perceived and treated outside the home. (2002: 41)

A confused (or I suspect sometimes just lazy) example of this 'not noticing ethnicity' is the anglicisation of non-European names, seldom with the pupil's informed consent.

School vision

Confidence and clarity about this paradox has serious implications for schools, especially mainly white ones where, as I have argued, there is less confidence about when noticing it causes offence and when it does not. One of the key difficulties mainly white schools face is lack of familiarity with dealing with race and ethnic diversity, whether in terms of being comfortable with the appropriate language, discussing difference with parents or pupils, or dealing with overt racism. This is not to deny the imagination or the conscientious work of many teachers trying to move such issues more into the mainstream of ordinary schools, as opposed to schools with high minority ethnic populations, but it is to recognise a basic element of the problem. In CPD work in white schools such feelings are frequently aired, as exemplified here by two responses to Cline *et al*'s research:

> The fact that you are asking me questions about it worries me because I find it quite difficult to think of a child as being different because they happen to have a different skin colour or their mother or father came from a different country to Britain and things like this worry me because I am having to think of children as different and I don't want to. (Cline *et al*, 2002: 42)

> I certainly think that within our department that we do extremely well and treat everyone as equals. Every one on their merits. There is no prejudice whatsoever that I have ever picked up here with regards to the different ethnic minorities. I think that is part of the reason that we haven't really considered that. We do a lot of result analysis. That is a big thing at the moment. We have never really looked at the ethnic minority. I know you are compiling data about how the ethnic minorities do at the GCSEs. We have never done that. Really it has never come to our minds because we do see everybody as equals. (*ibid*: 101)

The benign intention is clear, and most of Cline *et al*'s informants 'saw their school or class as trying to treat all children equally and playing down ethnic and cultural differences' (ibid: 95), but treating people as equals does not have to mean treating all the same, it may entail treating them differently; 'treating everyone the same' may really mean treating them as *if* they are the same when in some important respects they are not. Here, discriminating *between* need not mean the same as discriminating *against*. This is not a new idea to teachers, who of necessity discriminate between pupils all day long to try to meet their different needs. The trouble with race and ethnicity is there is such anxiety and ambivalence about their social and political significance that schools end up denying there is anything there at all. In practice this can end up contributing to the institutional racism explored in Chapter 2. This is another paradox: treating everyone as if they were the same to avoid being 'racist' can be part of the construction of institutional racism.

> [A teacher] who had worked in a more ethnically mixed school else-where in the UK was shocked by what he called the 'no problem here' attitude – a sentiment echoed by several others, along with references to tokenistic responses. The ignorance of pupils about other cultures was referred to, as were the negative attitudes of non-teaching staff and the common practice of anglicising 'foreign' names. (Gaine and Lamley, 2003: 90)

Cline *et al* found that many children 'play white' and 'many teachers minimise the significance and the value of cultural and ethnic diversity' (2002: 7). It is easy to see why more confidence is needed in this area by considering three orientations they found amongst minority parents and their children:

(i) Those who valued their ethnic identity and would have liked to see it expressed more fully and openly at school;

(ii) Those who valued their ethnic identity but were happy to develop and maintain a separate identity at school;

(iii) Those who considered that their future was in the UK and saw little benefit in maintaining their home culture. (2002: 51)

They add 'Our informants were heterogeneous in their attitudes on this central issue, and schools face a challenging task in attempting to respect this range of views' (*ibid*: 51) which is certainly true. In our Dorset study some teacher informants spoke to us because they were aware of inappropriate, patronising, insensitive or racist teaching materials or approaches. Young people also told us about difficulties encountered in certain lessons. Insensitively handled curriculum content made them uncomfortable. So did teachers 'shining a spotlight' on them, expecting them to make a generalised comment representing their entire ethnic group or, worse, another ethnic group of similar colour.

> But it is like you're sitting in class and they're, say, discussing other countries... and then sometimes they say something about another country and it's just like you know some people say such ignorant and crass things that is really annoying. Like they talk about Asian countries as being very backward, you just want to stick your hand up and say something....

> .... when we did about the slaves and stuff and you always think that everyone's looking at you like, they talk about it and people don't know what to do when they say like nigger and stuff, and even though they're not saying it about you I feel like everyone's like look-ing at you and thinking about you. .... and it makes you think .... you know out there some people still refer to us, different coloured people as like slaves and stuff ... so I don't like the lessons when they're talking about it. (Gaine and Lamley, 2003: 93)

It can be really hard to get it right. One mother of an eight year old described to us what was presumably intended as an attempt at inclusion:

> [The teacher] said 'We are having a talk about Islam and I asked your son to bring his prayer mat so if he can talk about Islam....' and I just looked at her. Really, to put pressure on a little boy to talk about Islam – it's not fair, she should not do that. I mean she can say my son is a Muslim and he does this and that, but she should do the talk-ing and answering the questions to the children. I told her I would come and talk to the children. My son might get bullied if he does what the teacher asked. (Gaine and Lamley, 2003: 93)

Courage is undoubtedly needed and mistakes will be made. The challenge will be entirely ignored in schools who hide in ethnic blindness as a solution, and related challenges are similarly avoided in striving for inappropriate colour blindness at times when to see it is appropriate.

A question of emphasis

Anyone familiar with previous writing in this field will know that much of it dwells on transitions in perspectives and orientations from the 1950s until current times. The bone of contention was about (and perhaps still is about) what we are facing and therefore how to deal with it, as summarised in this table:

Definition and terminology	Strategy in response
Increased cultural diversity and difference	Curriculum that reflects this
Ignorance and possible offence due to unfamiliarity	Attempt to raise awareness and sensitivity
Historic and persisting racist ideas	Curriculum that tries to challenge these
Inequality and injustice along racial lines	Policies and strategies that work against this

The point I want to make here is about emphasis. A good deal of this chapter has been about the presence of racist ideas and assumptions, and sometimes actions, in mainly white areas. My argument is that this should be our motive and starting point and that we should not confuse racism with ignorance; the problem is not that our young people know nothing but that they believe they know a lot, only what they 'know' is too often confused and heavily misinformed by bigoted and hostile myth. And to be blunt, some of our colleagues may, albeit politely, think in similar ways.

The overall stance of this book, therefore, is that shifting the curriculum towards information about other cultures will not address the most intractable part of the problem: a harder task awaits us in recognising and challenging prejudice and racism. It is too simple to say this has nothing to do with culture. I am not arguing it is inappropriate to have assemblies about Diwali or to invite in African drummers, but I am arguing that such strategies are insufficient on their own. Indeed, attractive and engaging though it may be to have African drums resounding through a rural primary school, if done in isolation the message of the drums may simply confirm stereotypical views. I return to this in the final chapter, by which time I hope the emphasis in the book upon recognising and responding to racism will have been sufficiently convincing.

Notes

1 The young people identifying themselves as: Indian, Jewish, Saudi Arabian, Chinese, UK/Swiss, UK/Greek Cypriot, Syrian, Pakistani, Indian, White/Caribbean, White/Thai, Caribbean, Kurdish/S American, Italian, UK/Iranian, Japanese, Arab.

2 See Chapter 5 for a full discussion of the social and political significance of 'black' as a self-description.

2

How did we get here?

Some past policy history

A national overview

Many texts chart the history of developing race equality work in schools (including the parent and grandparent of this book but also Klein, 1993; Massey, 1991; Tomlinson, 1990). This story does not need repeating in any detail here, although in the spirit of those not learning from history being destined to repeat it, I want to point out some critical themes. There are key lessons to be learnt about the different levels of change and action.

Perspectives about race and schooling, or educational responses to diversity, have almost always been represented as various overlapping stages. The first four are typically identified as:

- *assimilation*, a perspective focusing on minorities as immigrants with incompatible and probably inferior cultures; the educational focus was upon conformity and reducing difference, making the strangers less strange (1950s to the 1970s)

- *multiculturalism*, a perspective that sought to celebrate diversity rather than eliminate it, aiming to emphasise respect and mutual understanding, making the strangers less strange to 'us' (1970s and 1980s)

■ *antiracism*, focusing on issues of exclusion, inequality and injustice on the basis of race as well as culture (began in the late
1970s, largely driven out by government interventions by the late
1980s)

■ *reaction*, a rejection of critical stances about racism in the curriculum, some resurgence of assimilationist views about Britishness (from about 1982 until the Conservative Party lost power in
1997).

I would suggest two more. The initial stance of the 1997 Labour
government could be summarised as *market performativity*
(Gewirtz, 1997), the view that inequalities can be diminished by an
explicit and public emphasis on the comparative results of different
groups, with schools being held accountable. The aim seemed to be
to address race by making it disappear into a discourse about results,
so that school leadership, good teaching and high expectations in a
framework of inspection and accountability replaced much explicit
reference to former debates[1].

In 2005 this has shifted somewhat to a *race equality* stance, where detailed monitoring, obligatory policies and curriculum checklists
amount to a fairly coherent approach both to minority ethnic
achievement and a curriculum dealing with race for all pupils.

A white areas overview

What is notable about the first two perspectives is that they were able
to pass by white areas. The assimilationist immigrant perspective
hardly affected schools with few or no immigrants. The struggle to re-
place this with multiculturalism, a less patronising and more respectful approach that valued and recognised the cultures children
brought to school, tended to take place where there were such actual
children involved. The issue remained fairly abstract to the majority
of schools in the country because diversity had not yet reached them
in human terms or in terms of a wider view about social processes
and changes in Britain as a whole (Gaine, 1987; Massey, 1991;
Tomlinson, 1990).

This changed in the early 1980s. In some mixed urban areas the focus
upon injustice and racism had supplanted the 'softer' cultural diversity stance, and any such focus necessarily moves the spotlight away
from minorities to the majority, from the customs of black people to

the practices of whites. The Swann Report of 1985 gave added impetus to this by going beyond its original brief of looking at problematic African Caribbean achievement and calling its final report *Education for All*, declaring:

> We believe that a failure to broaden the perspectives presented to all pupils – particularly those from the ethnic majority community – through their education not only leaves them inadequately prepared for adult life but also constitutes a fundamental *mis*education.... (DES, 1985: 319; original emphasis)

In 1986 the Secretary of State for Education responded to Swann's comments about white schools by establishing funding for specific projects to develop work outside the metropolitan areas (Education Support Grant Projects – ESGs), so for a while there were structural incentives of funding, technical support and possible career advancement (all cited by Fullan, 1991, as common change catalysts). Within two years almost every English LEA had such a project, some employing half a dozen staff. Earmarked central funding was also made available for long courses for teachers in white areas. By 1988 many English LEAs had a written policy drawing attention to various aspects of multicultural education, to language issues, and to harassment. The majority of LEAs had an adviser/ inspector responsible for the issue. In principle, at least, *every* initial teacher education (ITE) course in the country had to ensure that students considered issues of race and culture. All this support provided pragmatic motives for LEAs and some headteachers to consider and to initiate change, and legitimised the growth of curricular work that examined discrimination, a less Eurocentric perspective in geography, questioning the canon of white fiction, even antiracist maths – which evoked from Margaret Thatcher the comment 'whatever that may be'. And it provided a receptive climate in 1987 for this book's grandparent *No Problem Here*.

In writing about the effects of the ESG projects, Tomlinson (1990) struck a positive note:

> An analysis of a sample of these projects suggested that project aims of raising awareness of the multicultural nature of society, challenging racism and promoting principles of justice and equality in all areas, were slowly being realised and the projects were acting as catalysts and agents for change in white areas. The projects were able to support those teachers and others who genuinely wished to

change their practices and attitudes, and the attitudes and beliefs of their pupils. They were having clear and positive effects on teachers, pupils, parents and others in areas where education for an ethnically diverse society had previously been considered unnecessary, if it was considered at all. The ESG project work ran parallel to the efforts of other teachers and educationalists concerned to make appropriate changes in 'subject knowledge', and to the values underlying this knowledge that might help to decrease white pupils' levels of mis-information, ignorance, intolerance and attitudes of white superiority. (Tomlinson, 1990: 170-171)

This is carefully worded, as were many of the formal briefs of the projects themselves, using words likes multicultural and strategically avoiding 'the a-r word'. Nevertheless, antiracism was at work, and the perspective driving many of the projects was that celebrating diversity was not enough.

In practice, social policy in this area is often the outcome of a balance of forces within government and a struggle to respond to contradictory pressures, so there are pendulum swings even when the same party is in power. There are also landmark events that determine policy for a while even if the government of the day wishes it otherwise. One of these was the urban uprisings or riots in the early 1980s reported on by Scarman (Home Office, 1982), that clearly revealed there was an explosive aspect of race that needed attention. This may have helped the positive reception Swann received in 1985, in hindsight another landmark or watershed in education's engagement with race. So things changed again, and the changes stopped development work in white areas for more than a decade.

While we can see developments in the mid 1980s moving apace at the level of the LEAs because they had considerable autonomy, supported for a period under Keith Joseph by the national state, by about 1987 the dominant perspective within the Conservatives had shifted. Swann's attempt to establish a kind of assertive multiculturalism alarmed those on the right of the party and by 1990 there was an explicit shift in central policy. The special courses were discontinued and special projects wound down. By 1993 no-one was left in post. The Conservative right were no longer prepared to tolerate the autonomy of LEAs pursuing radical agendas so they shifted power from LEA to school, partly representing this as 'freeing' schools from the ideological shackles of LEAs; they abolished the largest LEA, Inner

London, altogether; advisory work in multicultural/antiracist work was cut; and the requirement to consider race in ITE was abolished. In 1988 they introduced national control of curriculum content for the first time, in large part motivated by what they saw as a dangerous radicalising of the curriculum, not least with respect to race (Ball, 1994; Gaine, 1995).

The government had realised that the implications of Swann really were about 'all', and they set about rescuing British history from criticism and shame. In the construction of the National Curriculum there were clear examples in science, English, history, music, geography and art of direct intervention on the part of Secretaries of State to promote curriculum content which re-asserted a notion of Britain as a white, monocultural society, a move described by Ball (1994) as 'cultural restorationism'. The report of the committee established by the Government to advise on the multicultural element of the National Curriculum was never published – indeed it was shredded (Tomlinson, 1990; King and Reiss, 1993). Prime Minister John Major remarked that student teachers should learn how to teach children to read and write, 'not waste their time on the politics of race, gender and class'. This was actively supported in the press by a 'discourse of derision' (Ball, 1994), invoking the bogey of Political Correctness and the 'loony left' in order to, in effect, dismantle all the strategies which had been put in place to do exactly what Swann had argued was necessary. By the time the Conservatives had lost power in 1997 we were inhabiting a very different policy world from the earlier phases. LEAs had less power; the national state had more, taken originally with reactionary intent; the national climate and explicit national policy were firmly against antiracist work. Anti-racist work in white areas had become a 'legend in the hands of the few' (Carroll, 2003).

The advent of a Labour government in 1997 produced little immediate change, and indeed the market performativity approach is an aspect of New Labour clearly inherited from the Conservatives. Dependent as it was on middle class and floating voters, the new Labour government seemed anxious about appearing in any way radical in the mould of the often fictional but widely believed to be factual bogeymen of the loony left. So not a lot changed, certainly not the explicitly conservative chief inspector of schools, though he was much disliked by teachers.

The next landmark was the Stephen Lawrence Inquiry (Macpherson *et al*, 1999). This produced for the first time in Britain an acknow-ledgement from the centre of government that institutional racism was present in all key British institutions, and it gradually influenced nationwide requirements for a citizenship curriculum, Ofsted criteria about race equality that applied to all schools, more scope in the National Curriculum, and increased awareness of a need to address the issue of racism in ITE. In legislative terms it resulted in the Race Relations Amendment Act (2000), which made it obligatory for all public bodies everywhere – so all LEAS and all schools – to have race equality policies, policies that included detailed staff and pupil monitoring and a requirement to respond to and record racist incidents.

In this respect New Labour might be described at the time of writing as having an *education for race equality* approach. While they cer-tainly don't use the term 'antiracist', they support and initiate various measures in the curriculum, in training, in inspection, and in management priorities that focus explicitly on race and ethnicity. So it is targeted, it is explicit, and it is not derisive or undermining.

Something of this gradually shifting climate can be seen in some findings of Cline *et al*. On the one hand

> ...no school in this sample had a fully developed strategy for pre-paring pupils through the curriculum for life in a diverse society. The teachers we interviewed did not see any recent development at national level as encouraging a focus on this area of work. (Cline *et al*, 2002: 4)

But on the other hand they note the recent 'sharpening' of Ofsted's evaluations of school's strategies for promoting racial equality, ob-serving that:

> The comments during the feedback sessions suggested that this shift has had a noticeable effect on schools' experience of the process. During the earlier period neither the process of inspection nor the subsequent discussion of the report had stimulated thinking on pre-paring pupils for citizenship in a diverse society in any of the schools in our sample. But in the two primary schools that had been in-spected over the past year the picture was different. In one the management team had been asked probing questions on preparing for teaching and cultural diversity. The head said: '*We had to put our*

hands up and say: 'No, we haven't.' The action plan in that school covers this issue. The draft report on the second acknowledged what it was already doing but also gave significant attention to how the school might enhance teaching of *'the knowledge and understanding needed for life in a multicultural environment'.* (*ibid*: 106)

But no policy is simple and free of contradictions. No sooner did the Labour government begin to implement some of the imperatives from the Stephen Lawrence Inquiry than riots erupted in Bradford, Burnley and Oldham. They found themselves pulled between the demands of integration and unity and the demands of respecting equality and difference. These events occurred far from the white areas this book is about, but they influenced the national debate. While Labour had been more facilitative about religious diversity in schooling and has allowed state-funded Muslim schools to increase in number, they also grappled with tensions about the poverty and separatism that had developed in the rioting areas of those three towns. Asylum became a national agenda issue, in white areas too, spawning comments about 'swamping' from the Secretary of State for Education and designs for citizenship tests. All the same, it is a more favourable time in white areas than for many years.

Interacting levels of racism and change

This has been a brief analysis of shifts in policy and practice on a national scale, and some of the effects on classrooms. In theoretical terms this is a discourse about race at the *structural* level, where racism 'is part of the fabric of society, when black and Asian people are disadvantaged in laws, when other forms of racism permeate the key institutions of the state (Gaine, 1989: 32). Structural pressures and forces – like curriculum formation and assumptions and media agendas – are visited upon schools wherever they are.

> For most of the country, however, I would argue that structural *anti-racist* forces are fairly remote. All-white schools and LEAs are highly unlikely to be in the vanguard of antiracism because *they have no structural pressure or imperative to do so.* (Gaine, 2000: 70)

In a paper written during the last days of the Conservatives in the late 1990s (Gaine, 2000). I tried to summarise the network of factors that allowed or inhibited change over the previous couple of decades, grouped under structural, institutional, cultural and personal levels. The items listed in the structural level – national guidelines, policies, restrictions, the political and media climate – were pessimistic, almost all itemising retrogressive changes from the early 1980s on- wards and showing how they blocked change, whatever the impetus in the other levels. They also reflect the shifts and contradictions in policy during that period. Positive factors (italicised) frequently co- exist with negative ones, though it is noteworthy that during the Con- servative era the positive factors were bunched in the early 1980s and had largely vanished by the mid 1990s. The following table largely reproduces the text from this earlier analysis in the left-hand column alongside a comparison with today on the right.

Structural Factors Affecting Antiracist Education

Many of the suggestions in the right hand column opposite are con- testable, but they are intended to suggest trends. For example, I do not think that the presence of black boxers in the past did a lot for raising the general social status of black people nor do I think that sporting and entertainment success for the few is any substitute for fair employment opportunities for the many. But some individual Olympic athletes (like Kelly Holmes) have become widely acknow- ledged as representing Britishness, *some* media products by minorities have broken out of the ethnic ghetto and become main- stream, such as Meera Syall's work. It is too gloomy and pessimistic to dismiss all such examples as mere tokenism. Some features are always ambiguous and can be a help or a hindrance: local media coverage of a particular 'deserving' asylum case can raise awareness, as can a rabble-rousing article about Travellers; local racist activity may act as a catalyst for taking positive steps. Ofsted may have direc- tives and policies about what it must ask schools, but they have some way to go in always effectively interpreting the answers (Osler and Morrison, 2000).

We may not live in the best of all possible worlds, but the table argues that as regards structural influences on race equality we live in more favourable times than previously. The crushing effect of a negative national climate and negative national policies left many initiatives undeveloped and many unmarked graves of attempts in white areas to take race seriously.

Although the phases I listed at the beginning of the chapter are partly recognisable through the common assumptions of the time, the logic of describing phases is constructed in hindsight. In reality things

Conservative rule 1980s and 1990s	New Labour from about 1999 on
National climate	
Biological and cultural beliefs behind racism	Biological and cultural beliefs behind racism
Post Scarman anxiety	Post Macpherson concern
Ideals set out in Swann	
New Right and discourse of derision	Media/political focus on asylum and immigration
	Some media mockery of 'PC'
	Incoherent policy and focus on Travellers
	Higher status sporting and media presence
National Policies	
Courses and grants post Swann	*Race Relations Amendment Act (RRAA), hence*
HMI influence	
Flexible Section XI rules/later restrictions	*Ofsted guidelines and pressure*
	Requirements to monitor group achievement
Ofsted, TTA[1]	
Exam board interest	*Ofsted publications on achievement*
CATE and CNAA guidelines	
Teacher unions' documents	*Growth in DfES/QCA support documents*
	School and LEA policy requirement
	TTA 2000 standards
	New teacher unions' documents
ERA – NCC/SEAC – SCAA	
Emphasis on marketing/image/results	*Increased autonomy in curriculum*
Local climate	
Local political *support*/opposition	Local political support/opposition
Few catalysts in isolated/peripheral areas	*RRAA catalyst in isolated/peripheral areas?*
Presence of racist activity?	Presence of racist activity?
Local media stance and coverage	Local media stance and coverage
Local media stance and coverage	*Local media stance and coverage*
Local policy	
ESG project	*A few funded projects, e.g. in drama*
Race advisor in LEA	
Inset programme	*Some LEA RRAA training*
Attrition of LEA power/influence	*Slightly raised LEA profile through RRAA requirement to publish incident figures*

were messier than that and will continue to be; while there was more inexplicitness about race policy in the 1950s and 1960s (Kirp, 1979; Troyna and Williams, 1986) and rather more in the way of directing policy today, it is important to explore the scope for action and agency. Teachers are not robots without autonomy, and while they are constrained by many factors they also have scope for action. For most of us what matters is the change we can effect in our own spheres.

The story so far has sounded as if decisions were made in Whitehall or elsewhere and there were then recognisable outcomes in schools. Practising teachers do not operate at this level of influence and on the whole neither do practising activists. National policy seeks to determine many things, but there are institutional factors within every school and LEA that inhibit or support antiracist developments. There are also factors at the cultural level, both the culture of racism and the culture of teaching; and at the personal level, involving individual motivation and commitment.

The argument in Gaine (2000) is that nothing progresses unless change is possible at the same time at the level of structure, institution, culture and the individual, so in the table on page 42 I have substituted the 'new' column for the more pessimistic one in the original article. My purpose is to map out some connections and to suggest – optimistically – that scope currently exists for change at all four levels. Such change has more chance of taking root than when one level does not have to work against the others. I suggest the levels are interdependent but have some autonomy, so that one, for instance the structural level, does not determine the others despite its overarching power.

The other levels need some description. As the examples in the table show, at the level of the institution I mean LEAs and schools. The box labelled school micropolitics, for instance, will make sense to any teacher weighing up where support and opposition might be found. As I argued in 2001:

> In tactical terms, any change agent would have to examine their own colleagues for the different kinds of teachers identified by Ball as *believers*, for whom ideologies are important, *non-believers* to whom they are largely irrelevant, and *cynics*, who ridicule, reject or manipulate (1987: 16). Baldridge (1971) suggests officials, activists, attentives and apathetics, while for particular initiatives Lyseight-Jones

(1989) lists supporters, blockers, opinion leaders, don't knows, lag-gards and band-wagoners. As these labels indicate, in micropolitics *influence is at least as useful a concept as power*, and influence can be related to several features of an individual such as age or gender. The motive for egalitarian work is a problem. There are strategic, pragmatic, one might almost say selfish, motives for individuals (promotion, resources) or institutions (market advantage, profile): 'There are many reasons other than educational merit that influence decisions to change' (Fullan, 1991: 28). But there are principled motives: sometimes the motivation is provided by direct and ob-vious beneficiaries, and there are altruistic motives based on educa-tional principles and values. *Those who seek to persuade need to be clear which motives they are appealing to.* (Gaine, 2001b: 124)

Self-evidently this is also the sphere of operation of institutional racism, a widely familiar term following the Stephen Lawrence In-quiry, though still quite often misunderstood, involving both con-scious racism and unthought-out practices that have racist effects. There are at least five definitions, but in practice I think these are best regarded as partly overlapping and complementary. The first is the toughest charge, levelled by many against the Metropolitan Police, and the pervasiveness of the racism diminishes further down the list.

a) knowingly, key assumptions and attitudes widespread within the school are negative about minorities. Such attitudes are evident in terminology, common expectations, 'jokes' and procedures. In effect, as a matter of policy, the school discriminates.

b) unwittingly and unintentionally, attitudes and assumptions are expressed by many staff assuming the inferiority, inadequacy, strangeness, ignorance etc. of various ethnic minorities. Un-challenged but unconscious racism, present in individuals.

c) individual staff express their prejudices while the institutional culture ignores it, turns a blind eye, accords them the right to their own opinion, doesn't want to make an issue of it, accepts him/her as nevertheless a good colleague, is intimidated by him/her, or whatever, consequently does not prioritise the views, per-spectives or feelings of minority staff. Reinforced by occupa-tional culture, 'jokes' and teasing and professional loyalty and solidarity.

d) There is an uncritical and inflexible ethos deriving from 'the esta-blished way of doing things' which excludes minority ethnic perspectives, perhaps through cultural ignorance, lack of appreciation of or interest in barriers and disadvantages, laziness, unwillingness to believe anything critical of colleagues, naïve colour-blindness.

e) knowingly racist ideas or even practices are not endemic or widespread but may exist among a few members of staff, inevitably because schools are a cross section of society; the 'bad apples' theory.

The charge of institutional racism is still usually read as an accusation involving the personal conscious intention of individuals, but the possible manifestations of it above show that this need not be the case. Cline *et al* comment

> It was very rare indeed for children or parents to suggest that teachers' actions might be motivated directly by racism or to impugn their general fairness. At the same time it was recognised by many teachers as well as by parents and older children that minority ethnic children may often face covert or institutional racism. It appeared that in the schools in this sample this most commonly took the form of an indifference to or ignorance of what was distinctive about the experience of pupils from ethnic and religious minorities outside and inside school. (2002: 92)

It is really only the first item in the list above that involves conscious intention, the rest are about racist *effects*. This can become painfully obvious to someone engaged in raising the profile of race: the outcomes of a school's routines, whose opinions are sought and valued, how in the end decisions are really made – all these things can be thrown into relief. It can be in the silences, the ignoring of suggested revisions, the network of alliances and informal hierarchies where changes happen or get smothered at birth. The old adage that a working party is 'a blind alley down which new ideas are taken and quietly strangled' can be the stuff of institutional racism. Crucial also is the institution's motive for change; while institutions are not sentient beings they can nevertheless have motives that seem to support or squash some developments and ideas. Some of these issues are taken up in Chapter 3.

What *cultural* racism means in this context is the shared assumptions and beliefs held about other 'races' and ethnic groups – including the idea that there are such things as races. It feeds upon folk wisdom, anecdotes, so-called 'jokes' and shared, unchallenged assumptions and established ideas often rooted in the past. But it is renewed and reinforced by media and political discourses about conflict, difference and Britishness. It is likely to show itself in learning materials, implicit curriculum assumptions about what is important knowledge, whose art is superior, which music is the most advanced, which language is primitive, whose history should be the source of pride. These aspects of racism in white schools are explored in Chapter 5.

Personal racism, and hence change at a personal level, is the most obvious but the most sensitive level of work, since almost everyone in education is eager to deny any charge of racism and to take offence if they feel accused. Beliefs held by individuals contribute to the levels or aspects of racism already described, and looking at them instead may help to depersonalise the issue, but in practice it sometimes has little effect to say that everyone is at different stages on a journey towards countering racist assumptions and ideas and that we are all more or less affected by them. I might argue that we all have a racial frame of reference (Figueroa, 1984) through which we see the world because the world we live in is racialised, and that to a greater or lesser extent that frame of reference is a racist one. But such comments are highly likely to be *heard* as 'you are all conscious racists'. This problem is taken up again in chapters 3 and 4, though they permeated Chapter 1.

The following diagrammatical model, then, raises issues, asks questions and makes suggestions about why change is hard and what makes it easier. The italicising and repetition is removed because so many factors can operate either positively or negatively. It tries to summarise the complex and multi-layered nature of racism *and* antiracist work. It is a model of preconditions and processes. It aims to list the key elements in antiracist change, or the lack of it, grouped as responses to different aspects of racism. It summarises both the terrain and the kinds of change we're interested in. It represents the pervasiveness and intractability of racism, its presence in individual frames of reference, in cultural forms, in institutional practices and in structural conditions. But it is also a strategic map of action – or at least of the kinds of action which may produce change – as well as a map of sources of resistance and of inertia.

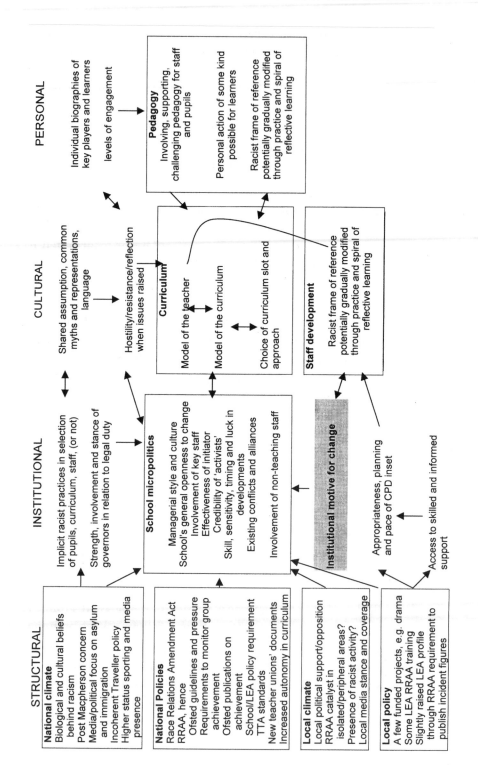

To counter the optimistic tone I have adopted, a sobering account of lack of progress in a shire county is provided by Carroll (2003), giving several warnings about an over-optimistic vision of change. Ofsted had said of the LEA

> Measures to combat racism in schools are not adequate. ..... the pro-duction of a statement of commitment to antiracist practices and the working draft of an action plan are due to be in place by the end of September 2001. This is too little and too late ... there is little evidence of support or guidance for schools around issues of diversity or deal-ing with racism. (Ofsted 2002, cited in Carroll, 2003: 152)

The CEO had expressed strong support for reforms, though Carroll's extensive contacts within the LEA suggested a variety of the forms of institutional racism were at work, particularly c, d and e, which pre-vented this happening. A minority ethnic member of staff given sole responsibility for furthering development was insulted, ignored, marginalised, starved of support, and left. An Asian trainer from the local race equality council was not invited to work with teachers again because they were 'just not ready for it'.

The story in that county is not a unitary one of obstruction and institutional racism, however, which testifies to the complicated and sometimes contradictory ways in which change happens. This led Carroll to devise a 'typology of engagement' to map the different levels of awareness and commitment to action of different members of the LEA.

1: Fully engaged	2: Vicariously engaged
Maximum contact with Black and minority individuals	Considerable contact with Black and minority individuals
Fully engaged with *issues*	Engaged with *issues*
Fully engaged with *experience*	Vicariously engaged with *experience*
BME individuals working in the field	Some white individuals in the field
3: Semi engaged	**4: Under engaged**
Limited contact with Black and minority individuals	Negligible contact with Black and minority individuals
Incomplete engagement with *issues*	Inadequate engagement with *issues*
Extremely limited engagement with *experience*	Negligible engagement with *experience*
Some white LEA officials	Very senior officials, some other officials, some secretarial and admin staff (white)

(After Carroll, 2003: 177)

This typology relates well to the large diagram above and can be applied beyond the LEA sphere, in that one may see where the presence of different levels of engagement can promote or inhibit change.

Notes

1 Though it is not enough in itself, there is something to be said for this. Effective monitoring of differential group achievement shows when specific groups are doing well or badly, and provides an inescapable agenda for Ofsted inspections, and some government initiated publications have highlighted trends that need addressing (Gillborn and Gipps, 1996; DfES, 2003). Such mechanisms may affect mainly white areas too: an LEA may have very few Bangladeshi pupils in any one school, but effective monitoring makes it possible in principle for aggregated results to show patterns across the LEA. The same is commonly true also of Travellers, the most common minority outside of urban areas and in some LEAs the most numerous minority ethnic group.

2 For those who have forgotten the general acronyms and the plethora of short lived bodies charged with implementing the government's educational agenda(s) in the 1980s:

1980s and 1990s designation	Current approximate equivalent
SCAA: School Curriculum and Assessment Authority	Qualifications and Curriculum Authority
SEAC School Examination and Assessment Committee	
NCC National Curriculum Council	
HMI Her Majesty's Inspectors of Schools	Office for Standards in Education (Ofsted)
ERA Education Reform Act	Seven subsequent Education Acts
CATE Committee for the Accreditation of Teacher Education	Teacher Training Agency
CNAA Council for National Academic Awards (awarded degrees)	Individual universities
ESG Education Support Grants	none

3

Cycles of productive change:
Practical steps to keeping race equality on a school's agenda

This chapter discusses school development in the light of the interacting levels which ended the previous chapter.

At a structural level – the rules and conditions created by major players like the government and the national media – the climate at the time of writing is relatively favourable. Compliance with the Race Relations Amendment Act (2000) requires every school to have a policy statement and action plan already. I am therefore assuming that in practice this chapter will be used for further developing and reviewing them, since the RRAA also requires regular review. An effective policy and action plan should be a cycle. Rather than a starting and an end point it is preferable to think of a cycle, probably annual, where various innovations and staff training/awareness-raising may have happened. This avoids the phenomenon of a burst of initial energy, perhaps from an advocate or someone really committed and involved in the subject, followed by grudging compliance in paper terms and formal but inconsequential annual reviews – what might be called institutional containment.

In a publication about policy development, I wrote:

... about the obstacles, hazards and misunderstandings which stand in the way of policies, because they are many. Policies are about change, they are not about static situations. Their production and formal adoption are critical stages in sharing and developing under-standing and commitment, and the whole point of adopting them is to legitimise and formalise the school's engagement with *something which needs changing,* or at least constant scrutiny. ... if guidelines, procedures, considerations and key ideas were widely shared and second nature, they would not need writing down or monitoring. It is because taken-for-granted assumptions, 'common sense' and first reactions are often not what produce the best longer term benefits for students that policies are needed. Policies legitimate certain con-cerns, provide resources to further them, and provide a basis for evaluation and refinement. (Gaine, 2001b: 117-8; original emphasis)

What should a policy contain?

A common problem with policies is that the more an issue is con-sidered the longer the policy gets. Someone committed to the subject of the policy either is, or becomes, knowledgeable about it, realises its complexity and how it reaches into many aspects of school life, so they make the policy ever more detailed with all kinds of important stuff included. The policy, while good in its content, then becomes too long for easy reference, looks intimidating to anyone who has to use it, relate to it or abide by it, so it gets filed in a drawer. This also happens because people don't really care, but that is not the only reason.

In considering practical guidance for race equality policy develop-ment in mainly white schools, my starting point is the Race Relations Amendment Act. But understandably, the law and some other general guidance documents and advice either try to aim at the whole country or implicitly have a multiracial area in mind. This book's intended audience comprises staff and governors of schools where there are few or no minority ethnic children and the parents of those few, so it has the dual function of telling parents what they might reasonably expect and could insist upon and also of outlining this reasonable expectation to staff and governors. Governors feature in this account because it is they who under the law have the legal duty to see that certain things are done. Heads have the legal duty to ensure that staff, parents and pupils know about the policy and that staff receive appropriate support and training. This is not something a school can choose to do or not do, nor can it claim that it does not have the resources to meet its responsibilities.

The Commission for Racial Equality's *Guide to Schools* is the most authoritative and thorough compendium of all that a race equality scheme needs to contain but it is lengthy at 29 pages and contains some formalities and some repetition, as well as examples which at times clearly do not apply to mainly white areas[1]. The next section of this chapter highlights the priorities for mainly white schools.

At root the law states that all schools have a general duty to

- take proactive steps to tackle racial discrimination

- promote equality of opportunity

- promote good race relations

and specific duties to

- have a written policy saying how the general duty will be carried out, identifying who is responsible and answerable for specific items. This requires an action plan but it does not necessarily demand a separate race equality policy – it can be part of the school development plan

- assess what impact all their other policies and procedures have on pupils, staff, and parents of different racial groups, especially on pupil attainment. This means reflecting on the way the school is run, which needs a bit of thought beyond the obvious

- monitor the effects of their efforts

- take reasonable steps to publish results of all this annually.

That, in essence, is the core of the legal requirement. There are many other sections in the *Guide*, but they overwhelmingly relate to minority pupils and staff and to potential disadvantages the school may impose upon them, especially with regard to achievement. I will return to these specifics later, but for general reference the full *Guide* is easily accessible on: www.cre.gov.uk/duty/pa_specific_education_schools_ew.html. A few case study examples relevant to white schools are cited at the end of this chapter[2].

Think of the majority

In a mainly white school it can be instructive to think out what the policy ought to be about if there were no minority children attending at all. Even with small numbers of minority pupils I would argue that the emphasis should not, on the whole, be about language provision, celebrating the ethnic diversity present within the school, catering for different religious diets, practices and sensitivities or dealing with specific kinds of bullying. It will cover these things, but they should not be the main driver behind the policy. The sole emphasis should not be upon the minorities present and their needs, but at least as much upon the needs of the majority. An unusual document was published by the National Association of Head Teachers in 2005, unusual in that while entitled *Race Equality and Multi-cultural Education* it has a significant focus on mainly white schools. It features authoritative case studies of schools in Cornwall, Dorset and white peripheral areas of Leicester, plus a section about Traveller children.

In practice, the presence of a specific child or group of children inevitably acts as a catalyst, so I don't want to be over idealistic or unrealistic. But in terms of meeting our legal duty and also in terms of providing a good education, the issue needs thinking about in general terms before a minority child – or a minority teacher – arrives -though certain specific skills, like supporting a bilingual learner are inevitably developed by practice. Consider how difficult it might be for, say, a vegetarian and devoutly Sikh man to arrive and work in your school. In reality, it is probably inevitable that that person would act as an informal trainer and awareness raiser, since none of us is perfect or fully aware and informed of everything, but there are nevertheless things any school ought to have thought out in advance, like expectations in assemblies. How unfair is it to put such a training role upon a child, expecting adults to adjust and adapt as the need arises rather than intelligently and pro-actively?

So the key question is what knowledge, skills and values about race should the school promote in its pupils and expect in its staff? How, in practice, will the school take proactive steps to tackle racial discrimination, promote equality of opportunity and promote good race relations irrespective of minority numbers in the school? There are some more specific points to be found in the resources and curriculum chapter, but I would suggest the school's broad goals in this respect should be:

- Having an openness and willingness to raise and discuss issues of race and race equality

- Giving a clear message of acceptance of difference and rejection of prejudice and discrimination

- Promoting positive and validating curiosity about difference

- Teaching age-appropriate factual knowledge to counter common myths and misunderstandings

- Developing age-appropriate teaching and learning about non-discriminatory language and stereotyping

- Having a questioning approach across the curriculum to Euro-centric bias and assumptions

- Making it clear to visitors, parents and any others in contact with the school that these are core principles.

These are what is meant in practice by the phrase in the Education Reform Act (1988) and repeated elsewhere: 'to prepare pupils to be full citizens in today's multi-ethnic society'.

Think of the minority

As a corollary of those goals specific questions would have to asked about minority ethnic pupils and staff – however few there are – monitoring ethnicity itself, specific needs, languages spoken, religious sensibilities, how they experience the school, and their achievement, but these flow naturally from the main goals above. There are two specific warnings in a recent major study undertaken about white schools in which white children outperformed their counterparts in more mixed ones:

> Children from Black Caribbean, Indian and Pakistani backgrounds in the same schools also outperformed their urban counterparts at GCSE level but not at the end of Key Stage 2. [They] shared in whatever educational advantages were available in these schools to the same degree as children from a White background in secondary school but not in primary school.

> In many schools and LEAs this data was either not available or unreliable, mainly because of uncertainties around the recording of pupils' ethnic background. (Cline *et al*, 2002: 6)

To take up the situation of new arrivals again, it is self-evidently much better for everyone if the goals are taken seriously before any minority pupils arrive. If they are, then a new intake of Traveller pupils, or two African refugees, or a Bangladeshi Muslim pupil, will not show up the flaws in a policy that exists on paper and nowhere else, neither will an Asian supply teacher or a black telephone engineer have to run the gauntlet of hostility as well as puzzlement. Perhaps it is analogous to an accident or a fire: schools need to be prepared so everyone doesn't panic and make things worse when something goes wrong. The DfES has published the best brief and focused guide to this issue: *Aiming High: Understanding the Educational Needs of Minority Ethnic Pupils in Mainly White Schools* (DfES, 2004). It is also instructive to consider the research questions of the study just cited into minority experiences in white schools:

- Are there differences in levels of educational achievement between minority ethnic children in mainly white schools and children from the same ethnic backgrounds in multiethnic schools?

- Do perceptions and experiences of the school learning environment and home support differ between minority and majority ethnic children in mainly white schools?

- How do children and young people from minority ethnic groups see/experience their lives in mainly white schools?

- Do children from minority ethnic backgrounds experience race-related harassment and bullying in the schools? What measures are taken to protect them, and what level of confidence do they and their families have in what is done?

- How do minority ethnic parents and children see the relationship between their home culture and the children's school culture and between their home culture and the ethos of the neighbourhood where they live?

- How do teachers in the schools view the education of children and young people from minority ethnic groups? Are there areas of knowledge, competences and resources that they perceive as essential but feel they do not have?

- To what extent do curricula, school ethos and classroom practices reflect the diversity of society as a whole and meet the needs and interests of all children in the schools, including those from minority ethnic backgrounds? (Cline *et al*, 2002: 2)

So race is relevant to schools that are racially isolated. But a large number of schools are also located in 'peripheral' or 'adjacent' areas (as defined in Chapter 1). For these schools, certain of the more general guides ask useful questions about admissions and monitoring. The ones I would recommend are:

> *Learning For All* (CRE, 2000);
> *Complementing Teachers* (Runnymede Trust, 2003),
> *Toolkit for Tackling Racism in Schools* (Dadzie, 2000) or
> *Promoting Race Equality in Schools* (Education Leeds, 2004).

Chapter 9 of the Cline study (2002) has some interesting quotes from minority parents and children about how they feel about religious and cultural recognition in school. These are worth reading since such voices are not always easy to access.

I've pointed out that one should not be misled into thinking a race equality policy only really matters in relation to minority pupils. But it would be unrealistic to expect everything to be thought of in advance in a school which, if it is the target audience of this book, has little regular experience with minorities. As I observed elsewhere:

> ...a change justified largely on principle or philosophy must be one of the hardest to make. In largely white institutions there are not visible beneficiaries of antiracism, except in the nebulous sense expressed by Swann of one's pupils emerging as better-educated people and citizens – a very long-term goal on which to expend resources and effort. .... In white areas there are unlikely to be realisable benefits in antiracism in the shape of more efficient procedures, fewer conflicts with or between students, higher results, more motivated students or better relationships with parents (indeed the latter may get worse, at least at first). In other words, the fewer the visible targets of a particular educational reform the more abstract it becomes. (Gaine, 2000: 73)

A good mechanism for annually reviewing the policy is to re-read the following sections of the CRE guide (see page 52), which relate to minority pupils and staff. Increasing familiarity with the issue can make old questions seem more relevant, and the school's composition may have changed – if only because of one new pupil.

This overlaps somewhat with a different CRE publication (see page 53), its *Code of Practice for Schools* (1999) which it quotes in the Guide for Schools (p.13).

- How do you make sure that pastoral support takes account of religious and ethnic differences, and the experiences and needs of particular groups of pupils, such as Gypsy or Roma, Travellers of Irish extraction, refugees, and asylum seekers?

- How do you encourage all pupils to consider the full range of options after they are 16?

- Do you monitor work experience placements by racial group to make sure there is no stereotyping?

- What support do you give to victims of racism and racial harassment through the school or with help from outside agencies?

- How do your staff create an environment where all pupils can contribute fully and feel valued?

- How does your teaching take account of pupils' cultural backgrounds, language needs, and different learning styles?

- How are different cultural traditions valued and made meaningful to pupils? Do you help pupils to make connections with their own lives?

- How do your teachers challenge stereotypes and give pupils the understanding they need to recognise prejudice and reject racial discrimination?

- How you collect ethnic data to monitor pupils' attainment and progress, and to set targets.

- How you plan to use ethnic data – for example on attainment, progress, exclusions, sanctions, and rewards – to inform planning and decision-making.

- How do you make sure your procedures for disciplining pupils and managing behaviour are fair to pupils from all racial groups?

- Do your staff use rewards and sanctions consistently?

- Do your strategies for integrating long-term truants and excluded pupils in the school consider the needs of pupils from all racial groups?

- Is your admission policy equally open to pupils from all racial groups?

- Do you monitor the admission process to make sure it is applied consistently and fairly to applicants from all racial groups?

Selected from CRE *Guide*, 2002 pp 20-22

a. Is the school making sure that its policies, for example on exclusion, bullying, the curriculum, parental involvement, community involvement, and race equality, are not having an adverse impact on pupils, staff or parents from some racial groups?

b. How does the school help all staff to develop and reach their full potential?

c. How does the school encourage all parents to take part fully in the life of the school?

d. Does the school help all its pupils to achieve as much as they can, and get the most from what is on offer, based on their individual needs?

e. How does the school explain any differences? Are the explanations justified? Can they be justified on non-racial grounds, such as English language difficulties?

f. Does each relevant policy include aims to deal with differences (or possible differences) in pupils' attainments between racial groups? Do the policy's aims lead to action to deal with any differences that have been identified (for example, extra coaching for pupils, or steps to prevent racist bullying)?

g. What is the school doing to raise standards, and promote equality of opportunity for pupils who seem to be underachieving and who may need extra support?

h. What is the school doing to:

(i) prepare pupils for living in a multi-ethnic society;

(ii) promote race equality and harmony in the school, and in the local community; and

(iii) prevent or deal with racism?

i. Is the action the school has taken appropriate and effective? Are there any unexpected results? If so, how are they being handled?

j What changes does the school need to make to relevant policies, policy aims, and any related targets and strategies?

(paragraph 6.15, *Code of Practice*)

Many of these points entail monitoring, the identification and recording of pupils' racial or ethnic background. While mixed schools have long been accustomed to doing this and in white areas practice is improving, many teachers are still uncomfortable about asking. Consequently too many pupils are recorded as 'unclassified'

– too many because it prevents any effective monitoring of attainment, but also because it demonstrates the misguided colour blindness argued against in Chapter 1. To do this monitoring well requires three elements: the first is understanding the need and the point; the second is practice, so it can be expected that nervousness or unfamiliarity initially causes misleading or inappropriate words to be used. The third element involves the range of practical information and knowledge that may be needed, and this is covered well on www.standards.dfes.gov.uk/ethnicminorities/faqs/.

Policy outline

To sum this up and incorporate some specific suggestions from the CRE[3], the outline of a policy should contain:

Background

A brief description of the local demography (obtainable from the LEA or www.multiverse.ac.uk)

An ethnic breakdown of pupils and staff (in a peripheral or adjacent area any contrasts with neighbouring schools should be noted).

Figures on racist incidents locally (obtainable from the police).

Goals

(as above), stating how they will be furthered and who is responsible for ensuring this.

Monitoring

...of curriculum goals for all pupils, ethnicity and related issues like language in relation to attainment for minority pupils; staff and pupil applications, who is responsible for collating information

...of impact and effect on other policies on behaviour, attainment, assessment, admissions

Shortcomings and breaches

What happens if goals are not met, there's a racist incident, a group under-performs?

Publication and consultation

Key details should be published annually to parents, via a newsletter, posters, part of a scheduled meeting. How will pupils be kept informed? How will parental views be gathered and responded to?

Despite my attempts to reassure readers that policies need not (indeed should not) be long and cumbersome, all these lists of questions and aspects to consider may seem to suggest otherwise. An alternative approach, which makes an effective policy seem realisable and possible, is to be found on pages 82-88 of Richardson, (2004b).

Training awareness raising, action?
Avoid a bland consensus

The seven goals listed earlier are easy to write, but they require much effort and change to bring about. The structural level gives them legitimacy in the form of the law, but they have to deal with personal, cultural and institutional racism to become actuality. Expect opposition. Even though the law and professional standards ought to remove race equality from the realm of 'just a matter of opinion', or a 'take it or leave it' option, a revised policy that really means something is unlikely to be achieved easily and without some argument. It is not enough to assume everyone will have a good level of understanding and empathy. Some will not, and they may silently oppose, perhaps resentfully, muttering in corners, or be overtly oppositional.

It is not that schools are staffed with conscious racists, as simplistic interpretations of institutional racism would have it. In their survey involving questionnaires to 217 minority ethnic pupils, Cline *et al* (2002: 31) found references to teacher racism were rare although they did occur (see also Gaine and Lamley, 2003: 92). But public attitudes about race are often either negative or confused and this has its impact upon cultural assumptions and personal, if inexplicit, racism. Some examples of public attitudes were cited in Chapter 1. To give another, a *YouGov* survey in 2004[3] found the following judgments of various groups by white people (see page 56).

Some of this clearly shows negativity. As for confusion, it also found that 27 per cent thought the average white Briton was either slightly worse off (16 per cent) or much worse off (11 per cent) than the

My opinion of this group is	Very high	Fairly high	Neither high nor low	Fairly low	Very low	Don't know
Recent immigrants to Britain	1%	4%	45%	20%	27%	3%
People seeking asylum in Britain	1%	4%	42%	21%	30%	3%
British born ethnic minorities	3%	22%	63%	6%	5%	1%
Travellers/Gypsies	1%	3%	35%	28%	32%	2%

average minority ethnic person. In fact, though it differs between groups, *all* minority ethnic groups stand a greater chance of being in low income households compared to whites; 50 per cent of Bangladeshi pupils receive free school meals, 42 per cent of Black Africans, 35 per cent of Pakistanis, compared with around 12 per cent for whites (Home Office, 2005: 21). While 40 per cent thought whites were generally better off, 33 per cent felt it was for people themselves to tackle their problems and not the government's responsibility.

In twenty years of running school workshops and training events I have not found teachers to be free of these kinds of ideas. I cannot say that these figures entirely reflect their views, though there may be some clues in newspaper readership. If they read the *Guardian* or the *Independent* they are less likely to hold the more typical views above, whereas 48 per cent of *Express* readers and 46 per cent *Daily Mail* readers are more than twice as likely to say that race and immigration is one of the most important issues facing the country. What papers do your colleagues read?

One therefore needs to be prepared for this when thinking of raising the profile of race equality. Few teachers will say that minorities are inherently inferior and there would be universal disapproval of *explicit* and crude racial discrimination, but to rely on this level of consensus would be to gloss over the negative, confused and mistaken ideas that circulate in the general population, ideas which will fuel misunderstanding and opposition to race equality work. So while there is a bland professional assumption that no teachers would do harm in this area, actually they could, whether because of complacency, nervousness, cowardice, unwillingness to examine their own attitudes, laziness or simply belonging to the canteen culture of schooling.

I am not suggesting that these wider social beliefs are explicitly fore-grounded and made the topic of public argument and discussion in school development, but they will be present whether one likes it or not. It may be worth tabling them, not with the expectation of any kind of resolution but to acknowledge their presence; to challenge complacent blandness while also recognising what people might really be thinking. One way of doing this might be to compile a selec-tion of such statements into a table (see page 58) for use at a staff meeting or any sub-meetings that may occur. Some responses to these statements are listed at the end of this chapter[4].

To use statements like these as a way of getting the real issues onto the surface would make for a stormy staff meeting which many people would not feel confident to manage, if only on the factual details. However, supposing one did do so, whatever the range of res-ponses the case will be made for taking action on race equality be-cause controversies will have been highlighted and almost certainly so will the racist beliefs that 'most people think'. One might also go back to the seven school goals suggested earlier, asking 'what is the role of a race equality policy in this context?'

Changing personal racism

This can be looked at in another way. From some research done on student teachers (Gaine, 2001a) I suggest four common orientations towards race, four different racial frames of reference (see page 59).

It would be an interesting exercise to be explicit about these potential views and make them a focus for discussion rather than act as if everyone has the same orientation to the issue, but this may be un-realistic in a couple of twilight sessions. Whether explicit or not, however, the task for individuals or people training and supporting them is to move towards the upper left quadrant. In Carroll's terms, this means to become fully or vicariously engaged.

The matrix on page 59 implies something about personal change, something that has had a bad press in antiracist circles. My view is that anyone who ignores the necessity of considering the personal level does so at their peril, and that a clear view of the aims and

TICK AS MANY COLUMNS AS YOU LIKE

	I THINK THIS IS TRUE ON THE WHOLE	MOST PEOPLE THINK THIS	THIS IS WRONG AND RACIST	I'M NOT SURE
There are too many asylum seekers in Britain				
Many asylum seekers are not genuinely at risk				
Immigration numbers are too high				
Immigrants are mainly dark skinned people				
Too many Asians refuse to accept British ways				
Asian women are oppressed				
Islam is medieval, narrow and repressive				
Immigration may be changing Britain's culture for the worse				
Many minorities are very prejudiced towards whites				
Many minorities are prejudiced towards other minorities				
Chinese and Asian pupils are likely to be well behaved				
Black pupils are likely to be badly behaved				
Black people are good at sport and dancing				
Black people are disproportionately involved in crime				
Travellers are pretty uncivilised				
Teachers have few prejudices and can be trusted to do a good job				
'Political correctness gone mad' means it's not safe to speak one's mind on these issues				

Structuralist

Antiracist There are groups of people in Britain defined by skin colour and often culture who have different life chances, and this racism must be recognised and dealt with in some way at school...	*Hostile (?racist)* There are groups of people in Britain defined by skin colour and often culture who have different life chances, but: we shouldn't pay attention to it (or) it makes it worse (or) that's just the way it is (or) that's the way it should be...
Anti-prejudice Personal prejudice is wrong, people ought to be thought of just as individuals. Doing so would bring about a kind of individualist harmony. Educationally, positive action should be taken so that this is encouraged...	*Indifferent (?racist)* People are just people, just individuals, and thinking in categories like race (or gender, or class) or the possible constraints or advantages which may flow from them is not really how I see my role as a teacher...

(left margin: take action; right margin: take no action)

Individualist

expectations of training is important. A good deal of educational work by teachers is private, individualised cultural reproduction, even if it takes place in classrooms. This is especially so in white areas, where racist practices affecting individual minority children or groups of them are less evident than attitudes and discourses – a common culture, a shared frame of reference about race. We cannot assume that guidelines or policies will produce real classroom change; teaching is personal so the person needs to be engaged. Personal change is slow, but it is necessary.

This matches accounts in the literature about educational change in general. Fullan, for instance, observes that 'Ultimately the transformation of subjective realities is the essence of change' (1991:36). Fullan also argues that wherever in the system change is initiated it is insignificant in classrooms unless materials are revised, there are new teaching approaches, and there has been an alteration of beliefs – the 'pedagogical assumptions and theories underlying particular new policies or programmes' (1991: 37). Cuban (1988) and Sarason (1990) argue that changes that go beyond merely improving the efficiency and efficacy of what is currently done are rarely successful:

> Most reforms foundered on the rocks of flawed implementation. Many were diverted by the quiet but persistent resistance of teachers and administrators... (Cuban, 1988: 343)

Training approaches

The model in Chapter 2 indicated that two elements are needed for this personal work to be effective:

- ▪ an involving, supporting and challenging training pedagogy

- ▪ scope for some kind of personal action must be possible for learners, so that a spiral of reflective learning occurs through supported practice.

Bhavnani (2001) summarises seven different training approaches, partly based upon the work of Luthra and Oakley (1991)

> Race Information Training
> Race Awareness Training
> Race Equality Training
> Antiracism Training
> Educational Approach
> Cultural Awareness Training
> Diversity Training.

Dadzie (2000) distinguishes eight, some overlapping with Bhavnani's categories, and both have the caveat that there are considerable overlaps between the approaches and they are not as distinct as they may at first appear. I strongly endorse that latter point, and suspect that few of these categories exist as pure types. Gaine (1987) explores the approach then known as 'racism awareness training' which fell out of favour by the early 1990s, partly because it was represented both by some antiracists and some right-wing critics as dwelling on personal white guilt. My experience of such training and acquaintance with many trainers led me to think this representation was a parody, fuelled by a wish by antiracists to stress the political and structural nature of racism and by some right-wingers in reaction to the discomfort they felt in recognising its pervasiveness.

Rather than categorise the different types of training that may have taken place at different times and potentially available now, it is more helpful to think of effective training for education settings as having certain elements, which in practice are always likely to be present to various degrees.

Cultural information and awareness: this kind of training dwells upon religion; dress; dietary rules and customs; cultural sensitivities, expectations and taboos; cultural norms about eye contact, conversational turn taking, gender and age patterns and hierarchies; the complexities of language use, common linguistic and metalinguistic 'crossed wires' and so on. It might be purely descriptive or it might be more engaging, so it might focus a good deal on deconstructing common stereotypes, or involve simulations where learners experience being cultural outsiders. In principle this kind of training could be relatively discrete from the others, but I believe it will not only have some overlap with others but also – even if only implicitly – have some element of affective engagement. This tends to be the kind of training white people think they would prefer, for reasons mentioned in this book: it locates 'problems' or misunderstandings mainly in 'them' rather than in 'us', and it identifies culture as the issue rather than racism. I have encountered this preference even in entirely white schools.

Racism information: this assumes the recipients are unaware of racial discrimination and its effects or that although vaguely aware, they may need periodic reminders. It covers the extent of discrimination and the experiences of minorities, extending from personal accounts to statistical evidence of inequalities and differential outcomes. In principle this targets the cognitive level, though since it can be uncomfortable to be faced with material about such things it is naïve to expect reactions to be purely cognitive and rational – some reactions will be emotional, others will involve the domain of morality. Such information is generally aimed at the majority population so part of the discomfort inevitably involves recognition of having a different lived experience.

Racism awareness: this shades into exploring how racism *happens*, so it should involve analyses of institutional processes, widespread cultural assumptions and beliefs and their reproduction, and how these can become embedded in structural factors like laws and the operation of key state institutions. It also, necessarily at times, involves people recognising their own racist ideas, assumptions and sometimes actions, and it also entails recognising that on the whole in Britain it is white people who have more power. It seems to me absurd to argue that because the recognition of this sometimes dawns on white participants the training can be condemned as individualistic, apolitical and focusing on individual guilt. I recall an exercise with head teachers focusing on how instant short-listing decisions may be made without thinking through the ramifications. A brief video clip showed senior staff looking through applications and one from a Jewish candidate being discarded with the comment 'This one's qualified, but I think she'd find it hard to fit in, in this area'. One of the heads present had a road to Damascus moment and burst out 'But I've done that!' and later talked about how bad it now made him feel. This was not the intention of the exercise, but it is a part of how institutional racism happens and how it is sometimes changed: not by automata implementing procedures with no responsibility for them, but by humans carrying out actions upon which they are able, given support, to reflect. The task is to engage with unintentional complicity with discriminatory practices, not expect a cure after which everything is all right.

Some research with student teachers makes a similar point. While the intention was to shift perspectives into the upper left quadrant of the matrix on page 59, the process of making that shift involved personal challenges.

> ...at the time I thought 'Load of rubbish', you know, 'He doesn't know what he's talking about...' and then I thought about it, and I thought about the people I'd come in contact with for most of my life and I thought well possibly, well you know I'm as guilty of that as anybody else. The course on race was very difficult because I had to really rethink my whole... all my ideas...

> Yes it was traumatic, because it stirs up the very feelings that you've got, your feelings might be wrong or something... I don't know, it was an eye opener... this course was actually delving into how you were as a person... it was uncomfortable because you have to re-examine yourself. (Gaine, 2001a: 101)

Antiracist: the relevant distinction from race awareness training is that this focuses upon action and change, but since the action is likely to be uninformed and ill targeted without both information and awareness, I am not certain this ought to be listed separately. Perhaps a distinction exists in who the training is aimed at, since an action focus implies managers and professionals, those with scope to take action. The focus upon action dwells less on simply ideas or attitudes and more on procedures, for example the implementing of monitoring and following up on its findings, or the evaluation of a curriculum and proposed modifications. Teaching is personal work, and the implementation of curriculum planning or minute by minute classroom management is not easily reducible to checklists and guidelines, so training that focuses solely on procedures misses important aspects of teachers' lives. This is discussed and exemplified further in Chapter 5.

Perhaps another way of distinguishing between these strands of training is *motive*, both the motive or goal of the institution – in this case a school – in setting up the training, and the motive being appealed to in the participants. If information is being provided there is an assumption that participants need it and probably want it; if awareness raising is the goal then volunteers are likely to behave differently from conscripts. In all cases the school's declared motive is important, but it could be presented as entirely instrumental – 'we have to do this so we can tick the Ofsted box', or principled – 'this is about educational values we cherish', or performative – 'this will help us raise test scores'.

Main emphasis of training	Institutional motives and expectations
Cultural information and awareness	– Prevent misunderstandings and clashes – Define any problems as cultural – Understand individuals and groups better
Racism information	– Remind of or highlight barriers, obstacles, different experiences
Racism awareness	– Understanding of processes and operation of racism, including own position in that
Antiracist	– Development of better practices that challenge or undermine racist outcomes – Legal compliance – Enhancing social justice – Raising specific performance levels

A proposed cycle of action

The diagram on page 64 suggests specific steps a school could take – all of which are supported by material elsewhere in this book. The only definite timescale is the policy review, which is meant by law to be carried out annually. The other elements could be carried out within a year, though the realities of the other demands upon schools suggests otherwise. In practice, therefore, the suggested items could form part of a three-year action plan as an absolute minimum, though some items – especially those with a curriculum focus – could occur often. These could be innovations developed by one teacher in one classroom, as long as they are shared with other staff.

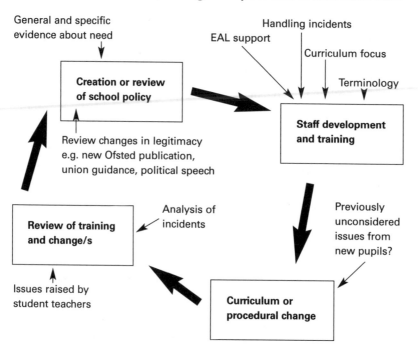

Training and awareness raising about incidents and name calling is suggested in Chapter 5. Terminology is explored in Chapter 4. Curriculum innovation is virtually impossible to cover in a way that will resonate with all age ranges, so the resources chapter is partly a list but also a series of questions which might themselves form part of an in-service/CPD activity. After these activities, or one of them, many staff may be more engaged with the idea of a race equality policy and willing to spend some time reviewing it – rather than it being an annual chore delegated to someone and internalised by no-one. Writing or amending a policy invariably seems abstract, whereas dialogue and reflection is a better way to learn and to improve practice. The existing policy will seem more relevant after doing some work on incidents or the curriculum and a consequent review provides an immediate affirming opportunity to show policy development.

Finally it is worth remembering that any diagram simplifies the messy ways schools develop in practice:

> School change rarely happens as neat, self-contained chains of cause and effect. Yet, the very act of presenting the change process through text, which must be sequentially ordered, imposes a particular 'logic' on the events that belies the uncertainty and the stress of the processes as they are experienced by the participants. (Gillborn, 1995, p100)

It is never as neat as I have suggested, though I believe the general pattern makes sense.

Notes

1 A particular reference that comes up frequently is to 'communities', which seems to me a very metropolitan perspective that leaves schools in isolated areas floundering. Travellers are present in significant numbers in some areas, though they comprise several different communities, and they most closely fit the image of urban groups living in proximity to each other with some sense of shared concerns. My own research in Sussex, Dorset and Herefordshire demonstrates that apart from Travellers the idea of communities in such areas is misconceived. The largest groups tend to be Bangladeshis and Chinese in the catering trade, who may be loosely connected through common needs for heritage language classes or a place of worship, but are also isolated geographically and because of their working hours. Other minority ethnic people are likely to be *individuals* with a huge range of ethnic backgrounds and circumstances, many of them mixed.

2 Some relevant case study extracts from the CRE's *Guide to Schools* (2000)

PROMOTING GOOD RACE RELATIONS

A small rural primary school with few pupils from ethnic minorities decided to encourage understanding and appreciation of cultural diversity by inviting a local black musician to the school. The musician, who specialises in songs and stories from different parts of the world, worked with pupils and staff, encouraging them to think about local and family connections beyond Britain.

The school also set up links with an inner-city primary school with a large number of ethnic minority children. The schools agreed to run parallel themes in certain subjects and pupils were encouraged to talk to each other on the internet, for example to discuss how they celebrate new year. Groups of pupils from each school also got the chance to spend time in the other school, on an exchange.

At the start of the school year, all staff in a secondary school were given a brief questionnaire on race equality and on the needs of pupils from ethnic minorities. A group of these pupils, drawn from different years in the school, were also asked whether they thought their different backgrounds were acknowledged and understood by the school and its staff. When both sets of answers were collated, it was clear that both staff and pupils thought there was

---

room for improvement in several areas. These were then included in the staff training programme for the next two years.

A school that regularly assesses its ethnic monitoring data on pupils' attainment found that pupils who had support in English as an additional language did well in some subjects, but not in others. To understand why, the school carried out a sample survey of bilingual pupils. It also surveyed a randomly selected group of pupils, for comparison. The pupils were asked about their favourite subjects and why they found some lessons easier to follow or more enjoyable. The survey found that it was important for all pupils – but especially for EAL pupils – to have a clear idea of the subject matter, and of their teacher's expectations and plans for the lesson.

Staff at an infant school realised that the school's only two Irish children were being called racist names. However, on reflection, the staff acknowledged that the children also used other kinds of name-calling. So they decided to tackle all name-calling and arranged a meeting with governors and parents and guardians to discuss the problem. The staff and some parents and guardians drew up a plan. This included:

making a list of all the names that were used;

attending classes to tackle the problem;

and using the records they kept to see whether their efforts had made any difference.

3 Another useful two page summary outline of a policy, developed by the journal *Race Equality Teaching* can be found on www.runnymedetrust.org/projects/education/ and a fuller but more digestible set of guidance notes than the CRE's can be found on the website of Portsmouths Bilingual Support service website www.blss.portsmouth. sch.uk/emtag/pdf/equalops.pdf (though in fact it's a guide devised in Stafford).

4 *Yougov* Survey For Commission For Racial Equality. 2065 white respondents and 816 non-white people. Respondents throughout GB online between 21 and 25 June, 2004.

5

There are too many asylum seekers in Britain	It's impossible to argue against this since to some, one is 'too many'. According to the Home Office, 72,430 people claimed asylum in the UK in 2002, about 20,000 were granted it. According to the UNHCR Britain takes 2% of the world's refugees. Over the past decade Pakistan and Iran have taken 2m each; Germany and Tanzania 1m. Britain is 19th in this list (BBC) and the 5th richest country in the world
Many asylum seekers are not genuinely at risk	...so they get refused asylum
Immigration numbers are too high	As with the similar view about people seeking asylum, what would just right be and by what criterion? The CBI insists the economy needs

	them and they help staff many public services, so it doesn't add up to blame them for waiting lists. If the point is really about colour or culture, see other answers.
Immigrants are mainly dark skinned people	It depends on when you're talking about. Until the early 1980s the largest immigrant group were Irish. The largest single settled group now is Indian, but for the past three years at least most immigrants have been white Eastern Europeans.
Too many Asians refuse to accept British ways	How do you know? A huge topic. An interesting starting point is to list some common 'British ways' and to estimate how many 'British' people follow them.
Asian women are oppressed	Unlike western women, of whom a Muslim woman remarked '...whose labour is cheap outside the home and free inside it, whose bodies are commodities and sales incentives in the media, who have no respect if they work and no self-respect if they don't, and who are conditioned to go to extraordinary and painful lengths to make their bodies palatable for men...'
Islam is medieval, narrow and repressive	How do you know? See Chapter One
Immigration may be changing Britain's culture for the worse	You'll have to specify exactly what you mean
Many minorities are very prejudiced towards whites	How do you know? Supposing it were true, are you also discounting 40 years of research evidence about white-black discrimination in, for instance, housing and employment
Many minorities are prejudiced towards other minorities	How do you know?
Chinese and Asian pupils are likely to be well behaved	How do you know? There's evidence to support this for Chinese pupils, for 'Asians' it's much too sweeping.
Black pupils are likely to be badly behaved	How do you know? The evidence about this varies with class, age, gender and specific 'black' roots. No reflective teacher should make such a statement
Black people are good at sport and dancing	This is one of the stereotypes black people dislike the most, since what often underlies it is a long-discredited 'scientific' idea that any differences are based in biology.

Black people are disproportionately involved in crime	What makes you believe this? Poorer people are disproportionately involved in crime.
Travellers are pretty uncivilised	How do you know? Another huge topic that needs discussing rather than responding to in a box.
Teachers have few prejudices and can be trusted to do a good job	So why did girls consistently under perform until the mid-1990s? Was it their fault?
'Political correctness gone mad' means it's not safe to speak ones mind on these issues	Define 'safe'.

4

Words, Concepts, Definitions, Terminology

Terminology is ultimately interrelated with the problems it describes. In a society so literate, so characterised by mass communication, so steeped in print, televisual and audio media, language is a crucial element of culture, social interaction and the making of social distinctions. Yet there remains some reticence about recognising the power of language, a reticence about making a fuss about 'mere words', being apologetic about wanting to insist that language matters. At the same time, it seems to me, many people in mainly white areas are uncertain, confused and cautious about the language of race. This chapter therefore sets out to

■ try to assert some definitions of two key concepts: race and ethnicity

■ discuss and undermine some stubborn myths and hence clarify some things about acceptable language and 'political correctness'

■ examine many of the specific words that are used specifically about race and diversity.

Race and biology: the legitimation of racism
'Race'
Academic and popular discourse about race is often vague about several related key issues and terms. In my own writing I have always

placed race in inverted commas to signify that it is a problematic term, but then in common with many other writers, have used it with reference to groups of people seen as distinctive primarily because of skin colour. In the British context these groups are currently usually referred to by the shorthand 'black' or 'black and Asian', but here and elsewhere terms like 'ethnic minorities', 'multiracial', 'minorities' and 'cultural diversity', are employed in discussing difference in relation to religion, language, lifestyle and dress, and extend to groups not necessarily marked out by physical differences, such as Jews, the Irish, Poles, Travellers and Italians.

In practice, however, at least up to now, skin colour has been a key element in what we think of as race in Britain, as discussed in Chapter 1. Colour has been highly correlated with discrimination and for various racist practices and beliefs, though the real hub on which racism turns is some alleged *attribute* of people of colour, which – if it exists – would be cultural. Nevertheless, I want to maintain that amidst what goes unstated, amidst the confusion, the blurring of terms and categories that bedevil this field, there has been a persistent undertow of biological assumptions. This informs 'common sense' ideas so it affects many pupils, students and teachers, so it has to be continuously challenged.

Race is a problematic term because it does not have the biological meaning many people think it has. Over a period of several years I have examined the definitions of race offered by groups of teachers and students, revealing considerable blurring of concepts from different kinds of discourse. Definitions tend to include notions of appearance and colour (biological terms), nationality (a political term), and language, religion and customs (cultural/sociological terms). For instance, when pressed, I have found that most respondents would loosely and inconsistently describe as a race: Italians; all black people; the Chinese; Pakistanis; Scots; and Jews, and confusion ensues in the cases of black Jews or Italian-speaking Sikhs. There is also considerable wooliness over what kinds of things may be genetically determined, like cricketing or singing talent, and how this might be linked to specific populations.

To take this latter problem first, folk wisdom attributes more to inherited nature between generations than geneticists do. Many assumptions about inheritance between generations are fairly

70

spurious – 'he's good with his hands, just like his father'; 'she's naturally reserved, but then so was her mother'. There could well be a genetic component to these, but the nurture element is bound to be crucial.

Folk wisdom is no wiser in its understanding of the distinction between physical attributes like strength, and psychological ones like placidity and 'being good with money', or relatively simple ones like a good singing voice and more complex composite skills like playing cricket or practising medicine. Some of these things are too complex or too new in human history to be genetically encoded and passed on from parents to children. To claim such attributes as biologically based and to go on to claim them as genetically shared within certain populations goes far beyond any scientific evidence, and in any case is simply not necessary, there are obvious and ample cultural explanations. Human 'racial' differentiation really is only skin deep. Any use of racial categories must take its justifications from other sources than biology.

Some idea of how biological assumptions effortlessly permeate public discourse is evident from two examples. The first is an article in the *Daily Express* of 9/4/92 (p.31) about women in the British royal family. Managing to combine racism, sexism and elitism, it speaks of the special qualities of reserve and coolness of British royal women and quotes a psychologist: 'Stoicism is in our genes. It's a national characteristic, something to do with being an island race...' thus giving the argument an apparent scientific authority. I cannot trace any research that would qualify the person cited to speak authoritatively on this.

Another example was provided by John Major in a speech about school sport:

> I don't regard sport – especially team sport – as a trivial add-on to education. It's part of the British instinct, part of our character. (reported in the *TES*, July 1994)

Instinct is a biological concept. The Prime Minister was not saying this is something developed in us culturally, he was saying it was *inborn*, innate. While these are both populist statements designed for specific consumption, they only make sense because they refer to and reinforce common-sense beliefs already in place. They are relatively inexplicit about racism, but that does not matter. They date from only the last decade but these beliefs are rooted in the nine-teenth century notion of essentially different 'races', each carrying a package of characteristics – some of them cultural — which correlate with, are signalled by *and determined by* skin colour. This extends even to cases where the physical differences are in part mythical, such as the Nazis' categorisations of Jews. Although a Polish Jew is much more likely to resemble a Catholic neighbour than a Spanish Jew, Nazis would resort to hidden biological features, 'natural' per-sonality attributes, and in principle – alarmingly – the two examples above do exactly the same thing.

I frequently encounter people who believe there is a series of signi-ficant and fixed patterned differences (genotypes) between human populations who look different (phenotypes). The most frequent 'evidence' cited is the differential performance of black sportsmen and women and their 'natural rhythm' on the dance floor. The under-lying and mistaken assumption is that the variant of the gene that confers dark skin and brown eyes simultaneously confers dense bones – 'black people can't swim' – or a type of tendon – 'black people are suited to 'explosive' sports' – or a special ability to get down and boogie. Thus various other characteristics – physical, psychological, emotional and intellectual – are 'read off' from the obvious one of colour.

The key issue here is the frequency of gene variants (alleles) that confer particular characteristics, and why certain alleles tend to occur together. For instance, it is common to think of African ap-pearance as a package involving particular facial features, hair type and dark skin, whereas in fact these are determined by different genes which are not tied to each other and which therefore vary independently. Any group which has historically been relatively isolated in reproductive terms will share a great many gene variants, so on this basis it is almost inevitable that a West African will have characteristic tight curly hair and dark skin, but the hair type is not *determined* by the skin colour, or vice versa. In principle it is quite possible to have tight curly hair and pale skin, a combination found in a small percentage of Norwegians.

Other significant physical attributes do not correlate with skin colour. Blood groups, for instance, bear little relation to superficially observable 'races': Eastern Australian Aborigines are more likely to be able to receive a blood transfusion from many Europeans than from Western Aborigines; organ transplants are as possible between a white Londoner and a Nigerian as they are between two white Glaswegians (see Dunn, in Kuper, 1975).

And yet, I was recently told by three separate sports scientists, no less, that there was a correlation between certain running abilities and race, black people being superior. Perhaps they were talking in shorthand, but the research they were referring to relates to a small area in the Kenyan highlands which has produced a remarkable group of long distance runners. The casual jump from this to 'black people' is really dangerous, but is born of simple stereotyping and unfamiliarity – they all look a bit alike so they are all more or less the same. If there were evidence that a small area of Scotland had a gene pool that produced good long distance runners, surely no one would attribute *all* Europeans with this ability, yet the slippage seems to be not just possible if black people are involved, but easy, almost automatic. Familiarity tells us that all Europeans do not look the same, some unfamiliarity and some prejudice tells us that all Africans do look the same, and also that in other ways they are pretty undifferentiated too.

We are only recently beginning to see some of the former patterns in particular sports beginning to change, but one has to look beyond the obvious correlations with colour to consider social explanations. These are usually economic: historically black people in the USA and Britain have been underrepresented in sports that need financial resources, such as swimming, tennis, motor racing, golf, polo, rowing, and over-represented in those which don't, like boxing, football, and basketball. The arrival of Tiger Woods and the Williams sisters on the scene only underline this point. If black people are so naturally good at dancing and singing then why have they been comparatively rare in ballet and opera?

Thinking of a fixed racial package of characteristics tied to an obvious one like colour is especially flawed when previously separate groups intermix, like the intermixing forced on slave women in the Caribbean and the USA by white overseers and owners. In these circumstances reading off other likely characteristics from skin colour takes no account of the European gene pool from which the father came – something that has surprised some American black people searching for their roots with the aid of contemporary genetic science.

The social value placed on skin colour categorisations is most starkly seen in societies with rigid 'racial' hierarchies. Being ostensibly white is not enough: physically a person may be indistinguishable from a group of whites, but if they are known to have one black great-grand-parent then there are places in the USA where the 'one drop' rule would still apply – one drop of 'black blood' and socially they are black. Away from their home area they could 'pass for white' until or unless it was known they had 'a touch of the tar brush'. In apartheid South Africa ostensibly 'white' people were regularly legally re-classified 'coloured' on the discovery of some piece of family history. Patricia Williams gave a striking example of the social nature of our idea of race in her 1997 Reith Lectures. An American visiting a Carib-bean island asked the prime minister how many of the population were white. 'Over 90 per cent' came the reply, much to the American's puzzlement. To explain, the Caribbean leader simply asked 'How do you decide if an American is black?' to which the American replied 'If he or she has a black ancestor'. 'That's how *we* decide if someone's white' was the prime minister's response.

The root of the idea of fixed racial characteristics lies in nineteenth century European science, which had the task of explaining the rest of the world with which Europe was in growing contact and the power it was exercising over it. This was particularly the case for the colonial powers such as Britain, France and the Netherlands since it is not possible to colonise people and simultaneously to treat them as equals. We needed an explanation for our dominance.

> The people of color of the rest of the world were thus variously seen as inferior, if not as animals, primitives, children, true or noble savages, or other non-and proto-humans... (van Dijk, 1993: p.159)

At one stage this ideological work was done by religion (see Banton, 1967) but by the mid 1800s a rationalist scientific spirit was increas-ingly contesting the ideological stage with religion (see, for example, Fryer, 1984, for the parallel developments in the New World of plantation slavery).

Out of this arose the crude division of the world's population into three main 'types': Caucasoid, Mongoloid and Negroid, and the belief that in some ways culture was determined by or at least related to these types. An example of this that survived until the 1980s was the widespread use of the term 'Mongol' for people with Down's Syndrome. This usage came about because nineteenth century scientists thought Down's Syndrome in Europeans was a throwback to an earlier more primitive form of human being, and that all Mongolians actually were 'Mongols'. Some equally explicit survivals of nineteenth century ideas are still around: the British as naturally inventive, or inherently reserved, or resilient – 'this island race'. The Jews are reputedly avaricious, the Gujeratis good at business, the Latin 'races' naturally more emotional or exuberant.

A study by Cashmore (1987) found ideas of this sort often articulated by his middle class respondents, such as a company director employing two hundred people:

> West Indian's intelligence doesn't seem to rise to that degree. Don't ask me why, unless it's that their initial intelligence isn't sufficient to absorb what's required. (1987:50)

or a Jewish surgeon:

> In spite of adversity, (the Jew) has triumphed. This, I suspect, is due to having a greater number of neurons, being brighter and learning to overcome adversity. (*ibid*: 58)

The explicit biological claim in the second statement has no basis in any known research, although in part this biological understanding of the word race is still with us in common sense because it is still with us in academic discourse. A notorious debate took place in the late 1960s and early 1970s, originally sparked off by Jensen in 1969 in the US and Eysenck (1971) in Britain. Their central claim was that black people had genetically determined lower IQs. Although this is scientifically untenable it was politically irresistible, so it ran and ran. It was resurrected in the UK by a special edition of the *Oxford Review of Education* in 1991, but with a much higher profile in the USA by Herrnstein and Murray's *The Bell Curve* (1994), which was discussed on chat shows, in *Time Magazine*, and showed up 'on the shelves of K-Marts all over the country' (Fraser, 1995: 1).

In the mid 1980s the Swann Committee engaged two Cambridge scientists to examine whether there might be a genetic component to the measured lower school performance of 'West Indian' children in British schools. By careful analysis of the figures they found no statistical evidence that could not be clearly explained without recourse to biology (DES, 1985: 126-148). What is even more interesting is that the question was framed the way it was in the first place: that those with Caribbean backgrounds were seen as a biologically different race who might accordingly have measurably different IQs. What really makes them different is the social value attached to their skin colour, not the skin colour itself. So it is dangerous for Jensen to argue that intelligence can be 'read off' from skin colour and especially so for Swann not to challenge the underlying logic – he did not have the benefit of Williams' telling point in her Reith Lecture. Herrnstein and Murray follow the same implicit logic, relying on the proven degree of IQ heritability and the average IQ score difference between American blacks and whites. As Gould (1995: 13) points out, they then commit the elementary error of attributing the difference to genetics, assisted, I would argue, by an underlying belief that black people are just different.

Thus physical phenotypes, taken alone, have no explanatory power in terms of social, cultural, historical or behavioural differences between groups of people. Indeed the classification and grouping of human phenotypes for this purpose was long ago recognised by most human geneticists and biologists as being an explanatory blind alley. As Troyna and Williams put it, citing the UNESCO Conferences of 1947, 1951 and 1964:

> The designation of the world's population into distinctive racial categories can no longer be considered a tenable scientific enterprise. (Troyna and Williams, 1986: 3)

What matters with 'West Indians', is not the physical difference but the social significance that is given to it. Van den Berghe offers this definition of a race:

> ...a group of people who are socially defined in a given society as belonging together because of physical markers such as skin pigmentation, hair texture, facial features, stature and the like. (van den Berghe, 1984: 217)

It is a social process not a biological one which accounts for why black people in Britain earn proportionately less than white people and for their disproportionate presence in some sports and many prisons. It is not genetically determined better vocal chords which explains the number of male voice choirs in south Wales, nor is it an inherited package of abilities genetically programmed into English middle class girls which accounts for their overwhelming presence in ballet schools.

Ethnicity: a social term?

This has been a substantial discussion and deconstruction of the biological myth of 'race' because I find it still so pervasive and dangerous. Discussion on ethnicity is briefer, though I hope to impart some confidence in the term 'ethnicity', since it is generally preferable.

The term tries to combine elements of what is in our heads when we distinguish social groups without going down the road of fixed 'racial' characteristics. This involves similarity and difference, most often along the lines of language, religion, geographical roots – so possibly physical appearance, and some customs to do with food, dress, family relationships and marriage. It also involves self-consciousness as a group, which may be internally generated or at least in part imposed from outside.

For instance, British Chinese people speaking different varieties of Chinese may in practice have been separate ethnic groups before migration, but in a sense become one ethnic group in Britain because their similarities, or perceived similarities, which distinguish them from the majority outweigh their internal differences. In other words, this self-consciousness as group members is partly defined by differences with others and partly by available identities. So in this case the similar geographical roots when combined with migration mean one of the boundary markers is physical appearance.

To take another example, there are many significant differences between Indians, Bangladeshis and Pakistanis in Britain, but they are often described as the ethnic group 'Asians'. Indeed there are significant differences within these three national categories. In Pakistan there are four regional ethnic groups: Punjabis, Pushtuns, Sindhis, and Baluchis. This has little resonance in the UK, however, since almost all British Pakistanis have roots in the Punjab, so in practice here Pakistani means Punjabi. But many Indians are also Punjabi, from the same region but just over the political border. They speak the same language as British Pakistanis (though write different ones) and have a good deal of shared history, though they practise different faiths. Are they the same ethnic group? Before the partition of India in 1947 one might have said yes, but whatever the commonalities one would have to say that now the two groups would be conscious of themselves as different. But this does not prevent them being classified together by white people 'from a distance', as it were. In Britain they become 'Asian', grouping them together with Bangladeshis, whose roots are a thousand miles further east, and other Indians who speak yet another language and practise another religion. This diagram, though not accurately reflecting scale or geography, may clarify the point.

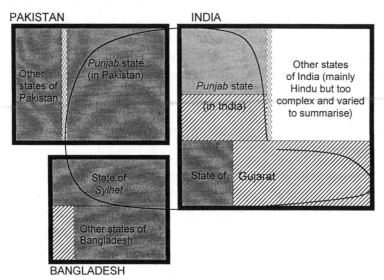

KEY

Muslim	
Hindu	
Sikh	
'Asians' in Britain	

'Ethnic group', therefore, is not solely and unambiguously a social term. It refers mostly to social features of culture but at times invokes physical appearance as a boundary marker, something that may make sense to those within the group as well as those outside it. All such boundaries are fluid and by their very nature cannot be regarded as absolute. Would an English Methodist moving to Wales, learning to speak Welsh and perhaps marrying a Welsh person become ethnically Welsh? Is a British-born English-speaking Christian of Pakistani descent ethnically British? If an Indian Muslim has a child with a Pakistani Muslim, what ethnic group is the child? These examples are not intended to argue that ethnicity is meaningless, only that it is not fixed, especially at the margins.

In practice, British society has tried to make sense of this through a mixture of social and biological categories, and the clearest manifestation of this is in the Census. Since the 1950s the largest visible migrant groups to Britain have originated from ex-colonies: the Indian sub-continent, the Caribbean and to a lesser extent Africa and Hong Kong. This has led to a broad but widely used three part categorisation of 'Asian', 'Black' and 'Chinese' and a Census question which asks the following:

What is your ethnic group?
Choose one section from (a) to (e) then tick the appropriate box to indicate your cultural background

(a) White

❏ British
❏ Irish
❏ *Any other White background*
Please write in below

....

(b) Mixed

❏ White and Black Caribbean
❏ White and Black African
❏ White and Asian
❏ Any other mixed background

Please write in below

....

(c) Asian or Asian British

❏ Indian
❏ Pakistani
❏ Bangladeshi
❏ Any other Asian background

Please write in below

....

(d) Black or Black British

❏ Caribbean
❏ African
❏ Any other Black background
Please write in below

....

(e) Chinese or other ethnic group

❏ Chinese
❏ Any other

Please write in below

....

Here the Office National of Statistics sought to count minorities in terms that made sense to the minorities themselves and that resonated with perceptions amongst the sometimes discriminating majority.

It did not have an easy task since the ways in which these issues are seen are not static and have changed at an accelerating pace in recent years. The inclusion of a 'mixed' category, for instance, reflected an awareness of increasing numbers of mixed relationships and dual heritages, the Census results later revealing that 1.2 per cent of the population categorised themselves this way. The inclusion of Irish as a category reflects the fact that the largest group of immigrants from an ex-colony are in fact from the Irish Republic, and they have often been 'disappeared' from people's mental picture of immigrants. Another aspect of the complexity of trying to map diversity and its relationship to inequality is British race relations legislation, which treats colour as a primary axis of discrimination, but also includes Sikhs and Jews as racial groups[1]. You can see signs of the confusion in the different 'ethnic' categories in the Census being initially biological/geographical, then the question asks for cultural background. This is not to criticise the ONS: it is simply trying to capture what is in our heads and our social practices.

In terms of the historically largest visible groups the following broad categories emerged from the Census:

		2001 Census data	
Asian	Indian Pakistani Bangladeshi	1.8% 1.3% 0.5%	3.6%
Black	Caribbean African	1.0% 0.8%	1.8%
Chinese	Mainly from Hong Kong	0.4%	0.4%

The groupings in this table reflect a number of assumptions. In common parlance 'minority ethnic' is widely recognised as shorthand or a euphemism for people who are distinguishable by skin colour: those in the table described as Asian, Black and Chinese. Because of a continuing pattern of discrimination in employment, housing, the criminal justice system and education, and a coded, implicit but usually present reference in immigration legislation, skin colour has been a key aspect of racialisation, a key signifier of difference.

The inclusion of 'Irish' in the census classifications reflects an increasing awareness of discrimination against Irish people, in fact a minority as large as several others in England at 1.2 per cent, and there have been further developments since the Census, with all public bodies monitoring staff appointments by ethnicity, all education bodies doing the same with students, and the inclusion of Travellers as an ethnic group.

A practical implication of all this is that schools have to monitor pupils by ethnicity, and many people feel uncomfortable about doing so. The flaws in colour-blind thinking are discussed in Chapter 1 and it has been my intention in this last section to unravel some of the ideas behind the terms. The following section considers some of the discomfort, the succeeding section some specific terms.

Myths about acceptable language

There is a problem with the word 'white'. In common parlance it seems to mean people of European ancestry, or even people of northern European ancestry, yet comparison of 'white' skin with white paper shows that the word is not to be taken literally. Why is this, and when did white people start describing themselves in this way?

According to the *Oxford English Dictionary* (OED), the first usages of white as a racial adjective coincided with colonialism and British adventures abroad. We find a reference in 1680 to 'non-whites' as 'the blood of Cain'; another in 1876 distinguished 'whites' from a 'Spanish Moor'; in 1726 white was used in Virginia to distinguish non-slaves and slaves, and 1777 as an official classification in a census in Tobago.

This usage should not be taken for granted. Why was 'pink' not used, since as a literal description it would have been more accurate? We cannot be sure, but it probably lies in the connotations of 'black' and 'white' and the preconceptions and assumptions of sixteenth and seventeenth British people about the darker skinned people they were encountering and, one way or another, dominating. In the nature of things these attitudes are not directly available to us, but it is clear that the first and subsequent contacts did not proceed on a basis of equality. 'Black' already carried all sorts of negative connotations in the language, and still does, arguably more so, the OED listing forty positive synonyms for whiteness, and sixty unfavourable ones for blackness. Thus its application to Africans served to symbolise for 'whites' many of the things they feared or disliked or disapproved of. 'White' had its connotations too: concurrent with the advent of 'black' as a racial term the OED points to usages like 'I meant to act white by you' meaning 'properly or honourably' and 'there isn't a whiter man in the area' meaning more honourable or decent. So partly from this colonial context and partly from before it, today we have a clear and striking contrast between the connotations of the words 'black' and 'white'.

Hall (in Palmer 1986) entirely misses the point of this when he goes to elaborate etymological lengths to demonstrate that 'black' did not begin to have negative senses at the same time as colonialism, that it has many neutral collocations, and that many of the negative ones have nothing to do with black people. The point is not the original use but the present resonances, the accumulated burden of social conditions which devalued blackness and inevitably enlisted language in the process.

So there is a problem with the word 'black'. It is not a term that all white people are comfortable with and at one time black people were not comfortable with it either. As a result, for most of the 20th century 'coloured' was the polite term for describing people of African descent in the USA and people of African-Caribbean and South Asian descent in the UK[2]. It was a euphemism, an apology for a skin colour linguistically and socially defined as undesirable. If people wanted to be offensive they would say 'nigger'; if they did not much care they might refer to 'the blacks'.

Though they should not be taken too simplistically, there are convincing studies which show many black children devaluing their own colour to the extent of denying it (Milner 1975, 1983; Stone 1981). Colour/status gradations were widely accepted among 'coloured' people in the USA and the Caribbean; skin lightening creams were on the market, along with hair straightening devices and European hair wigs, as seen on any early Diana Ross and the Supremes album cover.

In the 1960s African-Americans began to adopt the slogan 'black is beautiful' to rid themselves of the negative connotations of the word black. Being unable to sweep away the social distinction white people had created; black people went for redefining its significance in American social consciousness. This act of linguistic resistance was essential but it is scarcely possible to appreciate the scale of it. If white people today still have difficulties with the word 'black' how much harder must it have been for people defined and delimited by it, not just in the outside world but also, inevitably, inside their own heads? Skin-lightening creams were bought because the buyers too had internalised the idea of the undesirability of being black and the 'nicer' sound of 'coloured'.

By the late 1970s this cultural struggle had crossed the Atlantic and by the early 1980s generated a good deal of heat in Britain. For a while the word black had a certain limited applicability in the same sense as it did in the USA, namely to a group of people socially defined not by themselves initially but by the white majority. 'Blacks' were socially defined by discrimination in employment, housing, the criminal justice system and education; by the conditions of the Race Relations Acts which were designed almost entirely with them in mind, and by the operation of the Nationality Act which made it clear that they were less desirable than whites as immigrants. Thus 'black' in Britain became a socio/political term; it defined a group of people resisting a common relationship with society: the experience of racism on the grounds of colour. The acceptability of the word black grew amongst those to whom it was applied at the same-time as the decline in acceptability of the word coloured. As a youth says at the beginning of a film documentary in 1984:

> No black person who can truly say he is proud to be black can do so without having gone through a struggle, and a struggle of the hardest and most violent kind – within himself. (BBC, 1984)

The significance of the word was widely recognised as such by black people themselves from a range of backgrounds, especially in urban areas. If clearly used in this sense, it seldom caused offence – indeed most other terms would have caused more – and there was a consistency in meaning even when referring to groups as diverse as Ismaili Muslims from the Gujarat via Kenya and British born children of a Welsh mother and a Trinidadian father.

This is not, however, as simple as I once thought. Banton was probably right when he argued in 1987:

> My guess is that most white people in ordinary conversation would use the adjective 'coloured', whereas most white Labour Party activists, most white social scientists, most white people in the mass media most Afro-Caribbeans would make a point of saying 'black'. (1987:37)

There were considerable variations in different places around the country. Around Southall, especially at the time of high profile National Front and police activity, 'black' was what young Asians unhesitatingly called themselves. But there remained many Asians, and not just older ones, who preferred to be called Asian, or even coloured, but certainly not black.

Arguments continue about this, often beyond white earshot. Some entirely accept the common experience of colour racism but nevertheless see black as implying African. Some say this interpretation shows the persistence of a colonial mentality imposed by the British; others point to status distinctions between southern (darker) and northern (lighter) Indians, others are suspicious of a word which tries conveniently to lump together so many different groups. The debate has moved on for other reasons too. Increasing fragmentation, mixed and hybrid identities, the salience of class, gender and sexuality in how people see themselves, all militate against the relative simplicity of what Modood (1992) calls 'racial dualism'.

This is hugely determined by region, however, with London predictably in a different and much more complex cultural space than most of the rest of the country. Banton's observations from 1987 still ring true in some ways: many white people outside metropolitan areas remain unsure about terminology, not least the word black. One can often sense circumlocutions, evasions or hesitations sentences away from its possible use, and if the matter is discussed people frequently confess anxiety that black is a derogatory term, that it will offend, and so on. How this comes about, 40 years after African-Americans tried to say to white people they were proud of their blackness, warrants some explanation.

'Loony left'
In 1987 Goldsmith's College Communications Group traced a series of stories which emerged in the mid-1980s characterising some local councils, especially in London, as loony left. This extended beyond education to include the Greater London Council and its leader, Ken Livingstone, and at various times included the leaders of Haringey and Brent too, and a whole range of alleged 'policies'. Black bin liners were rumoured to be condemned as racist, teachers were allegedly not allowed to say 'blackboard', apparently only 'none-white' coffee could be requested in GLC canteens, singers of 'Baa baa black sheep' supposedly had to substitute green sheep.

In the past I used to raise these stories with various student groups, some in initial teacher training in Sussex and others on in-service courses around the country. Until the late 1990s most felt they could tell me confidently in which London LEAs they 'occurred', and many insistently added others they said they knew about. Even today, more than 15 years on, I still come across green sheep stubbornly wandering around in the educational landscape tripping people up.

The Goldsmith's study observes that of the ten stories they researched in detail:

> ...two ... proved to be wholly false. There was no event, order or instruction which could have possibly formed the basis for these stories. (1987: 18)

Of the rest, one came to be 'true' because nursery workers believed press accounts of a ban, and the others proved to have some connection with some event or set of facts, but were so distorted as to be unrecognisable. This point needs stressing: the stories were not true, the bans never happened, this self-evidently absurd policing of language was a myth.

How, then, did it come to be so widely believed? Clearly part of the answer is the extent and nature of the coverage. While not all national papers showed equal interest in these stories, several large circulation ones did: the *Sun* is implicated in nine out of ten stories, and the *Daily Mail* in six out of ten. *The Daily Mail's* sister papers, the *Mail on Sunday* and the *London Evening Standard*, were also prominent in a significant number of instances. In these papers and others, antiracists were described during this time as 'these dismal fanatics, monstrous creatures'; 'unscrupulous or feather-brained observers'; 'bone-brained left-fascists'; 'the hysterical antiracist' brigade'; 'untiring busybodies'; 'the multi-nonsense brigade'; and 'blinkered tyrants' (van Dijk, 1993).

The Goldsmith's study goes on to comment on the dissemination of this fiction outside London where it first pupated:

> A worrying feature of much of the press coverage is that many of the stories lifted from the national press or from news agency releases are reproduced uncritically in the regional press.... The journalists on these papers cannot easily check the facts of these stories, and a wholly misleading impression is consequently given to people living outside the capital. (1987: 19)

This was aptly demonstrated the same year at a conference in Chichester. One of the keynote speakers, then leader of Brent Council, referred ironically to the 'Baa baa black sheep ban'. Despite having a printed copy of her speech, a local reporter assumed he knew about this affair and reported her as defending the mythical ban (Gaine and Pearce, 1988).

Thus the individuals and the 'policies' became folk devils, easy touchstones against which people could interpret, trivialise and discount egalitarian measures. The agenda having been set, new stories simply had to press the right buttons to evoke a renewed reaction. In 1988 a single copy of an ILEA booklet about stereotyping in maths materials in a Wiltshire teachers' centre provoked national coverage about the 'loony left' and 'extremists' in the *Sun, Daily Mail* and *Sunday Telegraph*.

This is similar to the routine trivialisation of the women's movement by referring to 'bra burning'. While often invoked as a symbolic touchstone for feminism by its detractors, few know its origin. It dates back to 1968, when a group of women at the *Miss America* contest staged a small media event by putting their bras into a waste bin. At the time most bras were stiff, male designed devices shaping women into a pre-ordained template, a confining, conforming 'body armour' that women were expected to wear, 'those awful brassieres of the 1950s and 1960s that looked like pointed cones' (Lewis, 2004). One of the newspapers present touched up their photos, adding flames, and the legend was born, possibly confused with the anti-Vietnam movement burning draft cards. It may sound incredible, but what it tells us is the resonance of the event, the transgression involved in women asking for respectful and honest regard for their bodies, and the need of some sections of US and British society to undermine its seriousness, even 35 years later!

The same process applies to the myths about black coffee and the like in the 1980s. They served simultaneously to trivialise antiracist concerns and to warn of the threat to complacency they represented. And while the mythical bans are now largely forgotten or in the back of people's minds, it is striking how mentioning green sheep can jog people into remembering the 'facts'.

Political correctness

Following this onslaught, the word 'black' underwent an additional period of climate change. The uncertainty and anxiety produced by the loony left coverage was followed up by what we now know as political correctness. They were essentially the same phenomenon; both growing out of the politics of demographic change, though the latter was influenced by the USA in a way that the left wing councils of the 1980s were not.

According to Cameron (1994) the term was originally coined ironically by left-wingers in the USA, gently mocking their own preoccupation with getting the right political line on certain events and half-borrowing the term from 'correct lineism', a phrase used by the Communist Party. It may also originate in the English translation of

Mao's *Little Red Book* in which the words correct and political appear often. It was soon taken up, however, by the political Right, who sought to characterise it as a kind of leftist McCarthyism, a thought police, which

> ....if allowed to run unchecked, will curtail freedom of speech, deny common sense, threaten the foundations of family life and rewrite our literary and national histories until all notions of western values are denied. (Dunant, 1994: viii)

Or as Duncan Campbell (2002) put it, it was a 'masterly invention by conservative commentators of a problem which doesn't exist'. It played on the uncertainty, ignorance and some unwillingness to offend of many white British people. Just at the time when black people had started to become comfortable with the term 'black' for themselves, white people were pushed in the other direction by more media nonsense.

The nonsense and confusion arises from not critically considering the different nuances of 'black'. Sometimes the word has an evaluative content, a judgmental and almost invariably negative element. Thus black look, black day, black hearted, black magic, black mood, blackguard, blackmail, blacklist, blackleg, black market, black mass, the black sheep of the family and some black things with distinctly negative connotations like the cap worn by judges before pronouncing the death penalty and the flag flown by pirates. The exception is 'being in the black' at the bank.

There are, however, many phrases involving black which are not evaluative, including those contained in the loony left/PC mythology, so there is nothing racially offensive about a blackboard, black coffee or in wearing a pair of black trousers. The black sheep in the song is just a black sheep, not a bad sheep, and in fact some argue it's being asked if it has any wool because its rarity makes it more valuable.

The negative nuances to the word do not bother everyone black to the same degree, and it is unlikely that its original root is racial. Whatever its origin, the argument now is that it has a racial effect. It runs the risk of continuing the negative association of black with negativity and undermining the huge cultural work that has had to be done by black people to reclaim 'black' as something positive. There are those who argue reparations are due to black people for enslavement and its continuing destructive effects: the least we can do is allow the reclamation of a word.

Verbicide?

Probably beyond its wildest dreams the trivialising 'anti PC' campaign has worked. I have come across students who believe that 'folically challenged' is genuinely proposed as a polite term for people losing their hair rather than a joke coined (I believe) on a Radio 4 panel game. Small wonder, then, that they are themselves challenged when trying to unravel which words are offensive and which are not. Prompted by the obvious absurdity of objecting to 'black coffee' but nevertheless made anxious about it, many people in what we might call 'areas with milk' feel uncertain about when they might be corrected for using the 'wrong' term and understandably become resentful about it. This may not come out in professional conversation in case they are perceived as taking the wrong line but it has festered in private ones and has now surfaced in a kind of consensus against what people understand as PC, with the effect of removing or silencing much critical judgement. As Cameron points out, if asked 'Are you politically correct?'

> ... to say yes was to claim for yourself a definition constructed by conservatives for the express purpose of discrediting you; to say no was to place yourself among those conservatives. (Cameron in Dunant, 1994: 16)

I maintain that this struggle with language has to be worth it and is not completely new. An obvious example is 'nigger': at one time a common expression used to describe black people (even by black people themselves, which is another story). Such usage is found in Dickens, Twain, Byron, Joyce and Kipling, of whose book *How the Leopard Got its Spots* I have three different versions. The story inolves a formerly pink African getting covered in pitch and then being more successful as a hunter, sharing this with a previously tan coloured leopard by touching him all over with his fingertips. On the last page, when asked by the leopard if he wants to stay this way, the original version has the African saying 'yes, it's a very good colour for a nigger' (the later editions substitute 'African' or ' native').

Whatever one thinks of Kipling, I do not believe that he would have wanted the word to remain in current editions. It has changed from being the routine – if unthinking and demeaning – term for black people to being one which is universally recognised as insulting in the mouths or texts of white people.

This is not the same as banning words or omitting them from dictionaries. I share the view of the editor of the *Cassell Dictionary of Slang* that even though he as a Jew finds the term 'oven-dodger' for holocaust survivor deeply offensive, it has to be in the dictionary since its purpose is to record and map language (Groom, 2000). But it does seem to me quite right that 'verbicide' has been carried out on the sewing thread once catalogued as 'nigger brown' and that children are not taught the old version of 'Eeny meeny miney mo ...' nor that they grow up with some of the expressions that I did such as 'he wogged it' meaning 'he stole it'. On my Microsoft Word, if I type 'niger' the spell check does not offer 'nigger' as an alternative, though it accepts it if I type it in. It is a spurious and lazy objection to say that changing words does not change people's thoughts. In fact it might (see Gaine and George, 2000: 36-8) but in any case how can it not be right to watch what we say and avoid offence, or to address people and describe them in terms they find acceptable? If education is not the place to observe and reflect upon language I am not sure where it could be done.

Specific words that are used about race: a guide to walking on thin ice – and buying soft toys

By identifying and commenting on these I am trying to pull together hundreds of conversations on the issue over several years with people most often described by these terms, but this is not to say usage does not vary in different parts of the country, and it certainly changes over time.

> Language is continually evolving. The history of race equality and inclusion has also been marked by evolution of language and terminology. Some terms have fallen into disuse either because they were challenged over time or seen to be archaic or derogatory, being associated with a negative stereotype or an historical or implicit value system or hierarchy. Sometimes a term would fall into disuse as it insufficient for the purpose or context for which it was originally intended.

> No definition that relates to any individual's perception or self definition of their own identity is likely to fully describe the complex and subtle factors that contribute to that identity. These factors could in-

clude skin colour, language, national or regional origins, faith, culture, ancestry, family history in any or all combinations. (DfES, 2005, Standards website)

It is also useful to think in terms of Wilson's (1987) distinction between primary and secondary racial categories and what Modood (1992) calls 'mode of oppression' and 'mode of being'. The sense in which 'black' is most used by black people is in response to white society's view of them as simply 'not white'. Secondary categories are not necessarily to do with race at all; they may refer to religion, parental origin, nationality or culture.

Coloured(s)
Discussed at length above. Long declining in acceptability especially among those of Caribbean or African background, seen as a euphemism and offensive to many. White people should never use the term, especially if they are more comfortable with it.

Ethnic Group
As discussed earlier, this means a large in-marrying group of people sharing some cultural features, typically language and religion. If they are settlers or their descendants they are likely to have some distinguishing physical features in common too, but this is a distraction from the real meaning of the term. Everyone has ethnicity, not just minorities, so very loosely the English could be called an ethnic group, more clearly so could the Welsh.

Ethnic(s) or Ethnic people
A completely meaningless term, though widely used. It denies any ethnicity to white majorities and has rather patronising nuances of simplicity and primitiveness when applied as an adjective to handbags, clothing and art.

Ethnic minority group (s)
Technically accurate and can be used for all such groups or a particular one. Sometimes a bit of a mouthful, sometimes comes out like a euphemism. The sequence *minority ethnic group* is preferred by some people in the hope that it may discourage the ignorant usage above: it keeps the words 'ethnic' and 'group' together to stress that everyone has ethnicity, but some ethnic groups are minorities. English residents in Wales are a minority ethnic group, as are Welsh

residents in England. The DfES states clearly that it uses the sequence 'minority ethnic' for just this reason.

Black and minority ethnic
Sometimes abbreviated to BME, an inclusive shorthand for a huge range of groups including white groups like Irish and Polish people.

Visible minorities
A useful term to refer to minority ethnic people who may experience different treatment because of visible differences, most obviously skin colour. Tends to be more used by academics and writers than minorities themselves.

Minority group
Tends to have wider implications than simply numbers or race, for instance disadvantage or lack of power. It does not make sense when applied to women, but can obviously include other groups like gay men and lesbians, Travellers and disabled people.

People of Colour
Growing in popularity among... people of colour in the USA but has yet to catch on in Britain. It would have the advantage of including the Chinese and Vietnamese, for once, but 'visible minorities' does this. It may see only trivially different from 'coloured', but the difference lies in who coined the term: choosing it is different from having it imposed.

Black or black people
The most accepted term in current use for people of Africa and/or Caribbean descent. For the reasons discussed earlier some South Asian people would describe themselves this way too. Some black people prefer the word to have a capital letter when used in the political rather than the adjectival sense. The justification for its use is outlined earlier, but, alas, nothing is simple. Are the Chinese politically 'black'? The Arabs in Britain? In the end we have to accept there is not likely to be a single neat word that sums up the complex social relations we are dealing with.

Blacks

This can be used pejoratively. It depends how you say it: it can sound okay in a American accent but seldom in a South African one.

Black British

Fairly generally accepted depending on the context. It has the advantage of stressing that the people concerned are British; most people would see it as only including people of African and Caribbean descent.

African-Caribbean

Widely used and acceptable to almost anyone of Caribbean background with historic African roots (it has mostly replaced Afro-Caribbean probably because of the widespread use in the USA of the term African American). Those wishing to stress their African ancestry, whether born in Britain or the Caribbean are more likely to simply call themselves African.

West Indian

The term most widely used in the past for African-Caribbean people and still acceptable to many, especially older people born in the Caribbean. In essence it is an old colonial term derived from Columbus's mistake. And besides, the West Indies no longer exist in any tangible form except as a cricket team.

Jamaican

Fine if you know the person/people concerned are Jamaican or have roots there. It can be taken as ignorant or insulting otherwise since although amongst the original settlers from the Caribbean about half were from Jamaica, they, and Barbadians, Trinidadians, St Lucians etc, tire of the assumption that the other half did too.

African

Fine if you know the person/people concerned are African, just like calling white people 'European'. Favoured by some people of Caribbean descent who want to acknowledge their original ancestry but feel no particular ties to the Caribbean.

Negro/Neqress

Not welcomed, it is too close to 'nigger'. As Portuguese for 'black' it was originally meant to be neutral, and in fact was campaigned for in the early 1900s by an American black activist as a replacement for 'coloured', but uses change.

Nigger

It may seem bizarre to include this word as even a possibility, but I do so because of the puzzlement occasionally expressed by white people at the use of the word by black people (especially American rappers) amongst themselves and about themselves. At one time this could be described as internalised oppression in a similar way to using the word 'coloured'. If 'coloured' was the polite term used by whites who understood all the negativity of 'black' in their language, 'nigger' was sometimes deliberately insulting, always demeaning, but sometimes simply patronising. But...

> When used by a white person addressing a black person, usually it is offensive and disparaging: used by black people among them-selves, it is a racial term with undertones of warmth and goodwill – reflecting, aside from the irony, the tragicomic sensibility that is aware of black history. (Sawyers, 1998: 6)

More recently, most visibly in rap music but more generally a part of US black language, the N word is used between peers as a generic term meaning 'person', as a mild insult, and – confusingly for out-siders who don't reflect on it – as a term of pride and identification. As Webster's dictionary puts it

> [slang, Negro] originally simply a dialectal variant of Negro. The term nigger is only acceptable in black English; in all other contexts it is generally regarded as virtually taboo, because of the legacy of racial hatred that underlies the history of its use among whites, and its continuing use among a minority of speakers as a viciously hostile epithet.

This is no simple process, it having developed in several cities in con-texts very different from the UK, but this last element is about re-claiming the word, about removing its sting. Black Power writers used it in the 1960s to distinguish activists from others. In a country where despite decades of civil rights legislation black people still ex-perience the worst housing and employment conditions, race still carries huge social importance. Many people know that they are still perceived not as people but as 'niggers', so their use of the word in every day speech as a term of endearment with attitude in such a potent cultural form as music attempts to reclaim it with pride. Ironically, this then sells it back to white people who buy their music, who might copy the style and the speech patterns, but ought to be cautious about copying all the words. Some black people are concerned about this process, with white corporations making money while circulating the ill-informed use of a private code. Spike Lee is highly critical of Tarantino who uses 'nigger' 28 times in *Jackie Brown*. He uses it himself in his own films, but he's black.

Language is fearsomely complicated because it carries so much of the meanings of social life. It's not possible to have simple rules about social use or to reasonably object to its twists and turns. That's just the way it is. I have little patience at times with those who keep asking 'but how come it's all right for *them* to use the word when we can't' because the question fails to take account of how situationally significant and embedded language use is. It is never just words, it is often about constructing important social meanings.

Asian

Geographically confusing since it ought to include the Chinese, but in common usage it does not. Probably for this reason 'South Asian' has been increasingly used to refer to those originating in the Indian sub-continent, who come from several distinct regions in India, Pakistan and Bangladesh. For a while it was generally accepted by the people concerned, unless used in a context where the many differences between 'Asian' groups ought to be recognised, in which case it would be taken for ignorance at least. This has become more salient recently as some people of South Asian descent wish to distinguish themselves clearly as Muslims and others want to do the opposite. Consequently we can expect Asian to become a less accepted generic term.

British Asian

As with black British, states an important fact, therefore a better term than simply 'Asian'.

Pakistani/Indian/Bangladeshi

As with Jamaican etc, fine if it is accurate. Where possible specific terms show more knowledge and hence respect, thus Gujarati,

Punjabi, Sylheti, or Muslim, Sikh etc. Whereas there cannot be many people who do not know 'Pakis' is an insulting generic term for south Asian people, I have heard the argument that it is a harmless abbreviation when used to refer to Pakistanis. I have never met a Pakistani who does not find it offensive when used by white people, but something similar is happening as with the word 'nigger': an ironic reclaiming of the word by young British Asians. If an individual's roots are, say Indian, it does little to diminish the insult 'Paki' to respond 'I'm Indian actually', since the insulter doesn't care: that's the whole point of the word.

East African Asian
An important distinction: people whose relatives went to Kenya, Uganda or Tanganyika before World War II from some of the areas in India which later sent settlers to Britain. They are a diverse group, including Sikhs, Urdu speaking Muslims, Gujaratis, and Goans with a Christian Portuguese-speaking background.

Indo-Caribbean
The most accepted self-description for the Trinidadians and Guyanans or their children of Indian descent. Many were taken there as plantation labourers – not slaves – in the 1800s.

People of — — — — Background
A term that is deliberately general and makes no pretence at dis-tinguishing different sub-groups. It has the advantage of including their British born children. A bit of a mouthful but unlikely to sound offensive (unless the speaker is obviously trying to avoid saying 'black'). Including a word like background, roots, descent or heritage when referring to a person or group serves the important purpose of signalling something about identity without trying to define it com-pletely. It's not really accurate to call a ten-year-old British born girl a Pakistani, but she is of Pakistani background/descent/heritage; she does have Pakistani roots.

Immigrants
No longer an accurate term for the almost 50 per cent of black and South Asian people born in Britain, nor for their school age children, 95 per cent of whom were born here. 'Second generation immigrants' compounds the error, implying that 'they' still do not belong. In any

case, it is often not a particularly helpful term for describing people who have lived and worked here for up to 50 years. How about 'settlers'? 'Immigrant' technically includes white immigrants who outnumber black and Asian ones anyway, though it is seldom used that way. 'Economic migrants' is sometimes used pejoratively to refer to an alleged sub-group of 'bogus asylum seeker', but immigrants cannot win on this point: if they come for economic reasons they 'take our jobs' – though at many times in the past 50 years, including at the time of writing, Britain is short of workers. And if they come fleeing from persecution they are 'parasites'.

Asylum seekers and refugees

The former want long-term settlement rights and protection from the country they have fled to, the latter may be more temporary and wish to return home when, for instance, a war is over. Just as disabled people tend to prefer not to be simply described as 'the disabled', the phrase 'people seeking asylum' may serve to remind us that these are, after all, people like us.

Other races/Minority races

The problem with the word 'race' is that there is no such thing in the sense that it is usually meant. Scientifically or biologically speaking the significance of skin colour and certain obvious physical features is far less important than blood group and other, invisible, genetic traits. Skin colour's significance is entirely social, so really race is a social evaluation of a cluster of physical characteristics. For this reason some writers have always put the word in inverted commas to signify that it is one kind of term masquerading as another. Thus race relations or racism refer to the consequences of placing social significance on some biological facts that have no inherent meaning in themselves.

Cultural minorities

Technically exact, but in Britain cultural minorities tend not to be socially significant unless they are somehow tied up with the notion of 'race' and racists categorise cultures according to race in the belief that one determines the other. We should therefore beware of speaking as if cultures are the real basis for inequalities. As Madan Sarup (1986) said 'We don't have culture riots'. On the other hand, there are occasions where being aware of cultural differences between minority ethnic groups is vital. It is a code phrase, and generally understood as referring to certain groups – but is not the British aristocracy a cultural minority?

Half-caste

This term is widely disliked in the USA and in Britain. 'Mixed race' is often preferred, not in the (non)sense of being biologically half one race and half another, but in the social sense. Other terms that will not be perceived as offensive are 'mixed heritage' or 'dual heritage'. Some people of mixed parentage choose to call themselves 'black'. This may depend on how they are treated. It is no use saying 'No, I'm dual heritage' when someone calls you a Paki.

Gypsy

The word probably originated in the 1600s in the mistaken belief that the Romany nomadic people to whom it was applied were originally Egyptian, when they were actually of north Indian descent. By the 20th century it was always a pejorative term but as with some others it is more recently being reclaimed. In this sense it is used as a self-description, distinguishing Gypsy Travellers (both with capitals) from Irish Travellers, New Travellers, show and fairground people and bargees. In mainland Europe Gypsies are usually called Roma and seldom live a nomadic lifestyle.

And some observations on soft toys....

Although this is not about words it involves the very same processes for both black and white people, and is so often raised in the same discussions that I cannot resist discussing it here. This is about the gollywog, the last part of whose name ought really to seal the debate. The problem with them is well summed up by Peter Dobbie in the *Mail on Sunday*

> This slightly ridiculous floppy figure, a fantasy view of people in Africa, no less a stereotype than the bowler-hatted, pinstriped, con-stipated Brit which once epitomised our countrymen to so many abroad, is surely now no more than a toy. (*Mail on Sunday* 2001: 6)

Many people do not see the gollywog as only a harmless toy. The point missed by Dobbie is in his own words: the bowler-hatted Englishman was a stereotype circulated abroad in the past, a mocking one perhaps but a stereotype about a powerful country which once ruled 30 per cent of the world's people. The toy, on the other hand, represents the powerful's view of colonised and sometimes enslaved people, showing them as simple and childlike. The difference between the two stereotypes today is that is that some still want to circulate the gollywog here in the present, the *Mail*'s writer acknowledges it is an outdated fantasy image but does not recognise its currency still nor its offensiveness. To those who say 'it never did me any harm' I am often inclined to ask how they know, how they separate its effects from the many other influences which taught white British people they were superior to the colonial peoples we ruled. I wonder if it would be so easily sanitised if its original name was gollynigger, or how people would feel about a foolish looking Asian doll called a gollypaki.

Notes

1 It was also a legal category in South Africa, meaning of mixed African/European parentage.

2 The Race Relations Act 1976 as amended by the Race Relations (Amendment) Act 2000 makes it unlawful to discriminate – directly or indirectly – against someone on racial grounds. Under the Act, 'racial grounds' means reasons of race, colour, nationality (including citizenship) or ethnic or national origins. Racial groups are defined accordingly. For example, African Caribbeans, Gypsies, Indians, Irish, Pakistanis, Bangladeshis, Irish Travellers, Jews, and Sikhs are among the groups recognised as racial groups under the Act. In 2004 it became unlawful to discriminate against people on religious grounds, thus explicitly protecting Hindus, Muslims and other religious groups for the first time.

5

Racial incidents in white schools

We know that one of the key difficulties facing mainly white schools is a lack of familiarity with dealing with race and ethnic diversity, whether in terms of being comfortable with appropriate language, discussing difference with parents or pupils, or dealing with overt racism. This chapter is concerned with overt racism.

The social context of racial incidents outside school
Chapter 1 cited evidence about the experience of minority ethnic people in mainly white areas, and made observations about patterns in their experience nationally. This is important information because it shows the context in which racist incidents take place: not on a desert island where two strangers meet but in a society where we cannot help but be aware of prevailing images, stories, stereotypes, expectations and anxieties. These shape everyone's reactions to events and to things people say, minority reactions as well as those of the majority. When dealing with conflicts between pupils there is a tendency to de-contextualise them, to treat incidents as if no one comes to them carrying any baggage. The wish to de-racialise such events may be partly benign and done in hope, or it may be born of anxiety; either way it is a mistaken strategy. This is one of the occasions where we must notice 'race'.

As a reminder of some of the burden a minority child may bring to school, here are two accounts from Dorset mothers with Middle Eastern heritage:

> I have a neighbour a couple of doors away. The first look... you know what people are like ... sometimes you do know. We've been living here for the last fifteen years. When the children were very young they came to know this couple of children, they came upstairs and they were playing happily ... And I could see the parents don't like it. Their mother came round to the door downstairs I was, ... I was trying to welcome her with my face, smile, tone of voice everything, she didn't want to know. She wouldn't even look at me straight, she was just shouting for her children, 'Come down I told you ...' and she whisked them away and that was it. I was heartbroken for a few days, then I thought 'No, what can you do?' If they don't like foreigners they don't like foreigners because I can't even say they don't like me or us because we never had anything to do with each other. (Gaine and Lamley, 2002:40)

> I was in the car driving to go to town and it was very very slow, the traffic, and this car came on the other side. I slowed down and the other line of cars were slowing down as well, so this man said to ... a woman sitting next to him, 'Oh look, look at her she's covered up', and he actually spat at me. I couldn't do anything because the traffic went. I was shocked, I just had to turn around and go back home I was so upset. (*ibid*: 50)

This is local context; these are the kinds of things that happen to many minorities in largely white areas. One might say that at least the overt and unsubtle racism meant the mother knew where she stood with her neighbour. The second example indicates that one never knows when it might happen next. The uncertainty is compounded by accounts of attacks and harassment, which according to police data are more likely to occur in areas of low minority settlement. At the back of some people's minds they know they are a fairly visible target for race hate extremists. And not all targets of racist abuse are distinguishable by colour – and indeed some Muslims would say that colour is not what marks them out. Jews have intermittently been the subject of campaigns in some areas, cemeteries are quite often desecrated and pejorative stereotypes are still in popular culture (Runnymede, 1994; NUT, 2004).

But it is more usual for racism of a more uncertain and subtle character to be experienced. In our major study of minority experience in rural England we summarised the pervasive experience many people recounted as 'being marginal, being marginalised, or being targeted' in everyday life (Gaine and Lamley, 2003: 34). While some accounts went beyond being marginalised or subtly excluded and contained instances of explicit rejection, most people felt their 'antennae' have had to become well tuned. This Asian woman speaks for many:

> ...when somebody is racist you know. As a person of a different colour you know when people are racist... I have found the staff in that shop ... they see me coming and they will turn round and pretend they are doing something or chatting or something and make me wait, and I think its because of who I am. ... last Saturday morning she saw me coming, the assistant did see me coming, she saw me she couldn't have missed me. She just served somebody, and she saw me coming with purchases in my hand and she ... she deliberately turned round and for about a couple, three minutes or so was chatting to her counterpart over some display at the back. (Gaine and Lamley, 2003: 41)

Another respondent stressed that such behaviour was usually subtle rather than offensively explicit, but that 'he was able to tell' – for instance when a department store cashier refused to touch his hand when he paid. A white woman married to a Jamaican said her husband had become so used to the way people treat him that he usually no longer noticed, while she herself still got very upset. He did not consent to being interviewed saying 'Do I really have to dig all that up again?' to which his wife commented that 'he is just so worn down with it all'.

In recognition of the doubt minorities have to live with, we called a whole section of the study 'How Can You Tell?':

> You notice when you're in a shop and the person in front of you gets the full treatment. 'Would you like this Sir?' etc, and when it's your turn they take your stuff and that's it ... and then you wonder, just in terms of how you're treated. (*ibid*: 45)

> ... it depends what kind of stare it is. Some stares, I think half the men are staring because they like my black skin, and the others stare because they don't like what they see. ... but those who stare and I don't understand why they are staring at me, those are the ones I feel different with. Why are they staring? I wish I knew. (*ibid*: 46)

Though behaviour like this may not be obviously racist to many of the majority, it leaves little doubt in the minds of many people from minorities that they might meet racism anywhere, and that they can never be sure where.

Since September 11 2001 some school students with origins in Islamic countries have been on the receiving end of ambiguity of this kind:

> ... it's not always real feuds, it's even amongst friends ... there's always that underlying thing like name calling amongst friends ... it's quite friendly banter but there's always that underlying thing and it always seems more sinister when it's racially involved... If someone calls me an Arab there's nothing I can do, I just automatically think of my father, and it's my father I've inherited it from and I love my father more than anything so why attack someone I can't control... that's where it hurts most (*ibid*: 44)

The national context does not always help. We know there is a national issue about race; we know there are problems. At the very least we know there is a specific law to protect minorities from the discrimination they face and however positive their personal experiences are on a day-to-day basis, minorities do not tend to be active in seeking the repeal of this law. At the same time the national climate often highlights the issue of immigration control – usually code for keeping black and brown people out – which is often justified on the grounds of promoting good race relations. Put another way, 'of course minorities have to be treated equally, though they shouldn't be here in the first place'.

Inside school

It would be surprising if none of this seeped through the school gates.

> ...my children have suffered name calling and bullying – culminating in my two sons being beaten up last week because of Osama Bin Laden, according to the six boys who attacked them. They are all afraid to go back to school because the headmaster – although very sympathetic – cannot guarantee their safety. They fell in love with England when they arrived here but if they are too afraid to attend school they will never learn English and never become integrated. I brought them here to live in a country where they would be safe and have a good future – but fear due to racist attacks (especially since September 11th) is making them prisoners in their own home and

robbing them of the education that will give them a better future...I don't know what to do or who to turn to...(Gaine and Lamley, 2003: 95)

In their study of minority experiences in mainly white schools Cline *et al* found that 26 per cent of children 'had experienced unkindness or rudeness because they were different, because of their accent or because of the colour of their skin' (2002: 27). They mentioned name calling more often than white pupils as something they didn't like about school, particularly in primary schools. Although physical harassment was rare, over a third reported racist name calling either at school or on the way to and from home and half of this group described it as persisting over some time.

Our study of schools in the south west found a similar pattern. During interviews or via questionnaires to parents the commonest response when we raised the subject of schooling was to be told about incidents of racism by other children in the same school, together with the different ways in which the parents and the school dealt with the incidents. We focused in particular on the responses and actions of the pupils, their parents, and the schools concerned.

.... my daughter suffer a lot, I think she suffer more than me because she's English. She was born here but she doesn't look English ... There is no teaching about it in primary school. Kids are cruel they see something different and they will just go there and make a joke of her. There is no help, schools are not built for multicultural people, no ... Today there may be parents there who haven't got the same ability as I have or there may be children who never say anything to the parents. (Gaine and Lamley, 2003: 93)

Some schools deal with such matters well and in our 2003 study we found parents and young people who had raised incidents with schools in the past and felt supported and understood in the type and level of school reaction. In one, the head teacher was swiftly brought in. He met the parents of those involved and the boy who was mainly responsible was suspended for a few days and had to write an apology. The trouble stopped immediately, did not recur, and the interviewee felt the school handled the situation 'brilliantly'. Another interviewee mentioned the 'punishment' of getting the abuser to write a letter of apology;

> ...the school actually got one of the children to write to me a letter of apology and to my daughter so that was quite good I thought, it was quite, we've moved quite forward really. (Gaine and Lamley, 2003: 96)

One young interviewee told us with confidence that: 'My school would not stand racism'.

However, a common reaction from pupils was to tell no-one, especially teachers, in the belief that to do so would make matters worse. This reaction was also found amongst parents, in deference to their children's wishes, even when they had opportunities to inform teachers:

> If I wanted to do anything they would strongly be against it. They would not tolerate me going to a school to complain. They said if you come near us or if they make a point of it we would be bullied even more. (*ibid*: 94)

The strategy some adopted was to 'ride it out' – in one case for six months before they said anything to the school. One refugee family moved their son because of stone throwing and abuse, though they were disappointed that the school never asked why they were moving him. A final strategy was to confront the bullies themselves or delegate older siblings to do so:

> ... [my daughter] was called paki ... When she went to that school I went to see the headmaster and I also directly went to talk to this little boy who was the problem. I just dealt in my own accord I just went there and said, well I said to him 'You see the problem is with you is you're very very ignorant. ... I said if I ever hear anything again I will take you, little thing, and your family to court'. And he got really scared and left my daughter alone.

> During the years my boys did have difficulties at school with their names because they have different names, not English names. We had to deal with it, sometimes bullying as well. I don't approach the school with bullying I go and approach the parents myself. (*ibid*: 95)

It is unlikely that the schools would regard this as an appropriate solution, had they known about it.

While most schools' procedures understandably relied upon children or parents to report racist bullying, many families were unwilling to do so. In the Dorset study we received several accounts

where teachers were told about the racism that occurred i
schools but where no action followed. We were told by two stu
in the same school, whose parents did speak to the teachers a
the racist bullying they were receiving, that the bullying certainly did
not stop. They had been told that something would be done but
neither believed anything was: 'That's why I don't tell the teachers,
they don't do anything'.

One mother told us about how she battled to get the school to react
differently to racism:

> I'd said to the school that because I felt that they weren't supporting
> [her son] that I'd told him that if children said anything to him they
> could just say to them that if they continued he'd call the police be-
> cause it was a criminal offence to use racial abuse. Once I said that
> to the school it seems that they have taken it a bit more seriously. I
> don't know why... it should not have got to that stage before they
> did. (Gaine and Lamley, 2003: 95)

It took one person until she was in the 6th form to not only have the
confidence to confront the teachers about the racism in her school
but also to press for some action:

> Whenever I walk through corridors I hear prejudice, like Paki, Jew
> whatever. I'm bothered more about the younger kids ... so I did say
> to the head to try and reduce the amount of racism because ... is
> nothing, no counsellor, no assembly talking about racism. I think the
> school is very closed they don't like to accept the idea that there is
> racism going on in the school... (ibid: 96)

She recounted one incident in a classroom:

> ... There is this one boy who is very lippy and he was saying when
> you've finished your education are you going to go back home to
> Arab Land or Paki Land, and every one was laughing in the class and
> the teacher was just sitting there laughing. I couldn't believe it, he
> didn't even do anything. This boy was saying you f-ing Arab and the
> teacher just sat there laughing. The head of the sixth form was dis-
> gusted and I think something is going to be done about that I think
> teachers need to be educated about what goes on in the classroom.
> (ibid: 96)

Hamilton et al (1999: 6) found some reluctance amongst victims of
racial abuse to report incidents for fear of reprisals. This must be to
some extent connected with minorities' confidence, or lack of it, in

what the reporting procedures were and in the likely follow-up. This was echoed by Cline *et al*:

> Official procedures to reduce race-related bullying relied on children and parents to report any problems that occurred, but strong factors undermined their willingness or ability to do so. Consequently, in most of the schools some of the children and parents put little trust in the official reporting procedures. (2002: 4)

It may of interest to some schools to know that this featured as a factor determining school choice for some minority ethnic parents (Cline *et al*, 2002: 54).

Taking action because racist bullying is special

The parents' perceptions that support for their children is lacking is not a demand that schools should prioritise their child. It reflects the widespread ignorance of the impact of racist harassment. A study carried out in East Anglia almost 20 years ago showed that teachers' responses to children's complaints of racism from other children was a three stage denial: it's not happening; all right it's happening but it's not racial; okay it's racial but it's not serious (Akhtar and Stronach, 1986). One of the reasons why some parents and pupils experience a lack of support is that this denial still goes on. There is too little awareness that there is something distinctive about such interaction between children and that it merits special treatment. There are certainly similarities with other kinds of bullying and exclusion. Any pupil targeted for taunting or name calling can become very distressed by it and it can affect their school progress and indeed their whole development. They may also feel unable to tell anyone, usually because they fear that adults won't be able to help, however good their intentions. But racist name-calling has a unique power: it has more echoes in the real and adult world of discrimination and injustice than any other form of insult traded between children. I am not saying that racism is worse than anything else, or that it must always take priority, or that other people's struggles are worth less, just that it has a particular character.

To make this clear: let us compare three kinds of insult, choosing an insult relating to appearance, like 'scab face' for someone with acne; a sexist insult like slapper and comparing them with a racist one like nigger[1]. The core of the argument is more easily appreciated in discussion than in written exposition, so what follows might inform some CPD work, and skilled teachers might adapt it for their pupils' age range.

In working through this many times with many different groups, I have found no better way of beginning the discussion than using either *The Eye of the Storm* or *A Class Divided*. These are different editions of the same film of an American teacher who treated brown-eyed and blue-eyed children differently on two successive days, so they would learn about prejudice first hand (available to buy or hire from Concord Video in Ipswich: www.concordvideo.co.uk). The second one is more useful, as it shows much of the earlier footage and then one then meets the same children 15 years later and hears their and their teacher's commentary and reflections.

My own comments here are drawn from working through these questions with about fifty groups of teachers, interrogating each insult with the same series of questions. It is worth trying to score whatever consensus of answers arises, so that a conclusive and un-ambiguous 'yes' would score ten, whereas 'no' or 'almost never' would score one.

Is this insult commonly used between children?

This will vary with the children's age, but I think few would disagree with a 'yes' for all three words of abuse suggested as examples above. I discuss later how much it matters whether or not younger children understand the insults they are using. My point now is that they do use them.

Is this used between adults with the intention to insult?

Without getting distracted by the occasional affectionate use be-tween friends (e.g. 'Come on you old slapper, we're late for the disco') or the politicised use of 'nigger' between black people (see chapter 4) most adults agree that casual name-calling about appearance tails off with age, and is the province of the immature. But racist and sexist abuse, while clearly still engaged in by a minority of adults, is not simply playground language. Children do not necessarily grow out of it – unless they have help.

Might children use this insult towards adults?
Might adults use this insult towards children?

With the first question I have in mind the scenario in which a group of children call it out to a stranger in the street. With the second I am trying to imagine situations where an adult or group of adults in a public place might openly say 'scab face', 'slapper' or 'nigger' to a child or children they didn't know. I have chaired dozens of discussions about these two questions in relation to insults of these three kinds, comprising people with many different experiences and assumptions. On balance most people conclude for both questions that it is racist insults that are more likely to be hurled.

Does it insult only the individual targeted, or is it wider than that?

Being abused because of your race or ethnic group targets you, your family and probably the rest of the people from your religious and linguistic community. It may well be that the offender also believes s/he is speaking on behalf of a community. Being insulted because of spots does not even come close here. It is true that an insult about a girl's alleged sexual morals would generally be seen as an insult upon her family too, and such sexist insults might be seen as offensive to all women, not least because of the usual double standard that is employed. The distinction I would make, however, is that the whole point of calling a girl a 'slapper' is to say she is not like other girls; it is to single her out as different rather than to say that everyone she relates to most closely is equally stigmatised and undesirable. In this respect, such a sexist insult applies to an individual whereas a racist one applies to a whole group. In an important way it insults what a person is, not who they are or what they allegedly do.

Does the insult refer to something that is stigmatised out of school, amongst adults, in 'the real world'?

All do, but again to varying extents, and much discussion can be had here depending on which physical attribute is chosen for the first category of insult: wearing glasses, red hair, obesity, having ears that stick out, being very short or very tall. All have different resonances in the adult world. Some, like weight, have a gender dimension and others a racial one, such as 'fiery Irish tempers'. Nevertheless, sexist and racist terms are almost always rated by the groups of teachers who have worked through this exercise as carrying a greater adult stigma.

Does the insult reflect real material inequalities in adult life, like employment and housing?

Some recent studies suggest that attractiveness plays a part in career and other success, as does being obese, so there is no great dispute involved in stating that insults of all three kinds have real echoes in life. The point of discussion is whether they do so to an equal extent. Name-calling that has this 'real world' relevance continually re-creates racism, sexism or whatever attribute is being targeted, every time it is uttered.

Can the insulted individual do anything to change whatever about them is stigmatised?

I am not suggesting that they should. I am not claiming that having attention constantly drawn to one's acne is not serious because it will probably clear up in a few years, nor that being relentlessly mocked for having red hair is trivial because one can always dye it. Neither am I saying that the oppressive policing of girls' behaviour and dress is their own fault because they don't dress like nuns. The comparison with race or ethnicity, however, is worth discussing because race in particular is such a fixed category.

A working conclusion

It is striking that every single group of teachers who complete this exercise allocate a higher score for racial insults. This is not because I have persuaded them of it, but because of their own shared experiences and discussion. On the other hand, a study of white schools in 1999 found that:

> Teachers tended to classify racist incidents along with other forms of teasing and bullying, rather than as racist incidents as such, and racist name-calling was not taken seriously enough. (Hamilton *et al*, 1999:6)

This was echoed in the Cline study

> Some teachers ... expressed the view that race was often simply a characteristic among many others that could be picked out by bullies almost randomly *'like being fat or having red hair'*. No children or parents saw these insults in the terms used by that teacher... (2002: 78)

To repeat, I am not claiming that racism is worse than other verbal abuse, or that it must always take priority, or that other people's struggles are worth less. Many young people's lives are made a misery by the name-calling they suffer for all kinds of real or imagined attributes. But there is something different and special about racist abuse, and teachers ought to pause to consider this rather than try to persuade a minority ethnic child or family that their experience, while regrettable, is really nothing out of the ordinary.

To summarise, what is special about racist insults is:

- They are not just used between children, since
    adults use them towards other adults
    adults use them towards children
    children use them towards adults.

- Racist insults do not just insult an individual, they also insult the family
    they also insult others from the same background, the same religion, speakers of the same language
    they insult what you are, not who you are.

- Racist insults reflect stigma and real inequalities in the adult world,
    e.g. in housing and employment.

- Racist insults attack something the victims can do nothing about.

Considering a range of incidents
Racism and racialism
This is all to emphasise the point that racialised incidents in schools may be just 'ordinary' conflicts between pupils with a veneer of racial language, but they may also be *deeply* racialised. Troyna and Hatcher (1992) provided a useful distinction here between hot racism and cold. The former is name calling and the like in the heat of the moment, where the perpetrator draws upon the racist language available to all of us in the heat of temper and in searching for something suitably wounding. Such abuse may be heaped upon a best friend. The context still matters, since racist language is a powerful weapon precisely because of the context, but repairing the damage done by 'hot' expressions of racism is more straightforward than countering the effects of the deep rooted 'cold' kind, where racism of various kinds may be manifested in more calculating and systematic ways.

Some writers (e.g Bhavnani, 2001) revisit a distinction made some time ago between racism and racialism, reserving the former for more general manifestations in our institutions and culture and the latter for direct intentional expressions. It is a distinction worth making, though in practice the battle for doing so is probably already lost, the word 'racism' tending to serve both purposes.

Some example incidents

This section focuses on actual incidents in mainly white schools and possible responses to them. There is range of possibilities of which this first list contains the most obvious: they are in effect a racialised form of bullying:

- Physical actions like pushing, crowding, blocking someone's way and assault, the kinds of things normally associated with physical bullying

- Abuse of others' personal property in a racist context

- Verbal threats

- Derogatory name-calling, racist abuse, insults, 'jokes', innuendo

- Incitement to others to behave in a racist way including bringing racist leaflets, comics and racist internet sites materials onto the premises

- Attempts to recruit for racist organisations or groups

- Ridiculing people because of ethnic and cultural differences

- Written derogatory remarks and racist graffiti

- Racist phone or text messages, racist emails

- Wearing racist badges or insignia

- Racist comments in the course of discussion

- Refusing to co-operate or work with people because of their ethnicity, colour, religion, language.

Here are some examples of actual incidents. These can be used as tools in staff training:

> A black pupil from another class comes in with message, and a white member of the class starts making monkey noises.

There is a fight between a black and a white pupil. The white pupil says 'He called me paleface'. The black pupil says 'He called me nigger'.

A girl comes in late to a lesson and is directed towards one of the only two empty seats, which happens to be beside a black or minority ethnic pupil. She pulls a face and says quite audibly 'I'm not sitting beside one of them'.

An Asian boy is told by a white boy 'We killed loads of your lot yesterday, Saddam's your dad innit? It's time we got revenge for what you Pakis did in New York'.

You come into a classroom just at the end of a racist joke. White pupils are laughing; the few black pupils are not...

'Oh but Miss, racist jokes are funny – I mean Jasprit laughs at them, so they must be okay'.

You overhear a group of pupils in a corridor or the dining hall talking in offensive terms about 'gyppos' and 'pikeys'.

'Keep Britain white' is scrawled across one of the desks, and it's possible to pinpoint the time it happened to a couple of lessons.

You overhear in a crowded corridor 'I'm glad we haven't got any Pakis in our class'.

You overhear a pupil at break saying 'Don't be so Jewish, give me some of that...'

You receive some written work from a pupil that displays attitudes to ethnic minorities which are patronising at best, consciously racist at worst

A white pupil says loudly in class to loud approval from others that there are too many 'sponging refugees going on about their rights'.

A pupil loudly complains that an Asian girl is allowed to cover her legs in PE. 'Pakis are always getting special treatment'.

A video the class is watching happens to show in passing an Asian teacher with a class. A white pupils says 'My Mum says if I had a Paki teacher she'd send me to another school'.

Readers may immediately think 'that wouldn't happen in my school' and they may well be right. But the examples are all real and recent. Some took place in secondary schools, others in primaries, and there are details such as whether seating plans prevent the third incident from taking place at all. The point is not to feel comfortable that such incidents are remote and impossible, but to consider what a good professional response might be. It ought to be better than this:

> My other sons had trouble at school, the children saw a video about people coming to this country and making a home here. Straight after the video the children turned around and called my son a Paki. This kept happening so I went to the school but the teacher said, this is an educational video, I am sorry if your son found it difficult... And he did nothing. (Gaine and Lamley, 2003: 93)

It is usually the case that teachers are surprised when these things happen, so while the reaction 'that wouldn't happen in my school' is common, it is not always correct. Bullying by its nature often takes place away from teachers so it is not surprising that they may seldom hear overt and intentional racist remarks. Hamilton *et al* (1999) found that 'The extent and seriousness of racist incidents was underestimated by teachers and schools' (1999: 6). There is also some evidence that pupils or parents are not as confident as teachers think they are and can't bring themselves to report racist behaviour (Cline *et al*, 2002: 86).

Notice, by the way, that whereas the first list above mostly constitute racialised bullying, most of the example incidents cannot be classified this way. Typical lists of what constitutes bullying will include threats, physical hurt, damaging, hiding or stealing someone's things, teasing, name calling and abuse by various means) extortion, and exclusion, often with a repeated element. Definitions of bullying usually involve notions of a power imbalance, and that is certainly present in all the examples offered here, but bullying needs targets or victims, and they need not be present in some of the examples above for them still to be racist incidents.

One of the interesting features of several of these examples is that the perpetrators see no need to be covert. They do not see themselves as acting within the hidden pupil dynamics of schooling but as participating in a mainstream discourse. This is part of the context discussed earlier; without such a context the examples above have no meaning and no power.

A CPD exercise

When asked 'what would you do?' about incidents such as these, most teachers opt for a short-term response. Rather than thinking of an instant response it may prove more effective to adopt an initially more demanding strategy and consider the incident in four steps:

1. What are the underlying assumptions?
2. What are the power relationships involved?
3. What might be a good short-term response?
4. What would be your long-term response?

When using this exercise the examples should be modified to fit the age range and circumstances of the school, and the group should be allowed to choose their own example from the list offered. That way they will choose whatever is most salient to them. It works well to have the group read out all the incidents aloud, so everyone hears them before making a choice of which one to focus upon.

I will consider the last one in the list as an example: a video the class is watching shows in passing an Asian teacher with a class; and a pupil says 'My Mum says if I had a Paki teacher she'd send me to another school'. There is a lot of context we don't know: the pupil may not agree with her mother and be seeking support from the teacher; she may be a disruptive pupil deliberately trying to produce a re-action; she may be African (or Jewish). These would all be background factors militating against interpreting this as a 'simple' racist incident, but let us for the sake of analysis proceed on the assumption that the girl and her mother are white Anglo Saxons, that she seems to be signalling agreement with her mother, and that she does not typically set about annoying the teacher to disrupt the class. The other scenarios are all feasible, and would make equally good CPD discussion points, though in my experience it is all too easy for a group of white teachers to deflect attention away from majority attitudes by constructing this episode as prejudice between two minorities – it's much more comfortable.

The chart opposite shows what might emerge from a discussion of this incident, although the value of this exercise lies not in presenting such a 'worked example' but in teachers working it through themselves.

Underlying assumptions	Power relationships	
It is acceptable to express such overt hostility	offending pupil	minority pupil/s
	class	offending pupil
It does not matter if people are offended by this particular issue if class contains minority pupils	class	minority pupils
	class ⟷	teacher
It is okay to use the word Paki in class	teacher	offending pupil
	teacher	class
At least some of the class will agree	teacher	minority pupil/s
	mother	teacher
There is something undesirable about Asian teachers	school	mother
Being Asian is more significant than being a teacher		
Her mum has the right/power to take such action		

Short term response/s	Long term response/s
Reprimand on use of 'Paki', insist on apology to class	Check details of school policy
State disagreement with mother, move on, speak later	Ensure staff of all kinds have training
Ask what anyone else thinks	Consider specific contract with all parents
Engage in wider discussion, stopping original lesson	Examine positive role models visible and accessible in school: staff; assemblies; posters; displays; learning materials...
State legal employment and anti-discrimination rights of minorities	
Signal that the comment will be followed up	Enhance pupil involvement
Convey support/empathy to minority pupils in class	Tackle issue in Circle Time
Report and record after lesson	Review incident log regularly
Consider letter to offending pupil's mother	Publicise stance on incidents
Set up some one-to-one work with offending pupil	
Consider letter to minority parents, informing them of incident and response	
Tell colleagues about it	

There is no simple blueprint of set responses that 'work' in situations like this. It is one thing to reflect carefully upon all the ramifications of an incident; it is another to respond instantaneously in a way that could not be criticised later. Huberman's (1983) summary of the key demands in teachers' daily lives throws this into sharp relief:

- ■ *Immediacy and concreteness:* Teachers engage in an estimated 200,000 interchanges a year, most of them spontaneous and requiring action.

- ■ *Multidimensionality and simultaneity:* Teachers must carry on a range of operations simultaneously, providing materials, interacting with one pupil and monitoring the others, assessing progress, attending to needs and behaviour.

- ■ *Unpredictability:* Anything can happen. Schools are reactive partly because they must deal with unstable input – classes have different 'personalities' from year to year; a well-planned lesson may fall flat; what works with one child is ineffective for another; what works one day may not work the next.

- ■ *Personal involvement with students:* Teachers discover that they need to develop and maintain personal relationships and that for most students meaningful interaction is a precursor to academic learning. (Huberman, 1983: 482-3)

The summary characterises the enormous complexity of classroom life, which those outside classrooms seldom appreciate. Good practitioners have to develop intuitive responses to a huge range of situations so that they become second nature.

Checklist of responses

The less frequent and less familiar a situation the less likely it is that there will be a practised and confident response, so a slightly formulaic 'script' and some discussion when something happens is needed. This is one of the reasons why policies exist: they partly express intent and partly provide guidelines. The aspects of school life where there is consensus and shared good practice are precisely the aspects where policies would be very easy to write – and by the same token scarcely necessary. So even if, indeed especially if, such things seldom happen and are unexpected, the law is clear that all schools have to have a policy that responds to racial incidents, This means teachers must think about the steps to take and be prepared to respond. Working through many different kinds of incidents with dozens of groups of teachers has demonstrated that some key steps *must* be taken.

Try to decide if anyone thinks the incident is a racist one. This may sound odd, but the 'truth' could be in the eye of several beholders. The Report of the Stephen Lawrence Inquiry defined a racist incident for reporting and recording purposes as 'any incident which is per-ceived to be racist by the victim or any other person' (1999: 328). So if you think it is racist then you should act; if you don't consider it racist but an Asian pupil thinks it is you should still act. If another person present, adult or child, shows that they believe it is a racist incident then you should at least pay attention. Doing so takes away sole res-ponsibility from the child who has been treated badly. If their English is not good they may not recognise sarcasm or even clearly offensive language; if they are new to the country they may not be clear about levels of 'acceptable' teasing.

This definition tends to raise the temperature in all-white training settings because of the power it gives minority ethnic children or parents to define and name an incident in a way that might not accord with the perception of a white teacher or head. The same applies in other settings, such as those involving the police service.

The majority population simply have to live with this discomfort and get used to it. For decades now what counts as a racist incident has been defined by the majority white population and for decades minorities at the receiving end have had little choice but to live with their experience being denied or defined away. Those who feel threatened by this power to define might reflect on what it must have felt like to be insulted, and then be told that they hadn't 'really' been insulted at all, that they had imagined it, or that offence had not been intended, or that it was only a joke, or that they were over-sensitive, that they had no sense of humour, or 'I suppose we'd better not ask for black coffee', or 'that's just the way we talk here', or that they were not included in the general negative comment because 'they were okay', or that children say these things but don't know what they mean, and so on, and so on. For a while at least, until some listening skills have been improved, we in the majority are going to have to accept the boot being on the other foot, and not expect to be the authority on what counts as racism and what does not.

However, this power to define is about initial perception not final judgement. The definition gives a duty to take the perception seriously, to record it, and to investigate it seriously; it does not give the last word to the person who has the initial perception.

Though it is relevant, intention is not the defining issue. It doesn't matter whether or not a six year old calling someone a n***** really knows and understands its offensiveness any more than it matters if they understand what calling someone a c*** means. It doesn't matter if a thirty six year old intends puns on a foreign name to be demeaning if that is how the puns are experienced. There are some useful comparisons with sexism: many women are tired of being told 'I didn't mean it offensively' by men, as if it excuses their sexist remarks.

Identify and respond to the needs of the person victimised or targeted, if there is one. In this case, any Asian child present has had a word used against them that they are highly likely to find extremely hurtful and insulting, especially when a classmate's mother has said adult Asians are not fit to teach white people. You may think the girl did not really know what she was saying, but the point is the effect not the intention. The girl and the rest of the class all need to learn that. The range of possible responses to support minority children present is wide and will vary depending on the incident, so it would be fruitful for a school staff to discuss several possibilities. Effective support might well entail at least informing parents about the incident and the action that has been taken: doing so will help gain people's trust. Cline *et al* found

> Schools were more likely to win the confidence of minority ethnic parents and children in their ability to deal with racism when the head teacher personally was seen to deal with such matters firmly themselves and to provide a lead for others on the issue. This confidence was enhanced when care was taken to inform victims and their parents of the outcome of any follow-up to a report of racist behaviour. (2002:5)

Be seen by the class/audience to be taking it seriously. Experienced teachers have a repertoire of ways of conveying this. At times a few words might suffice, at others you may need to spend some time on the incident. Deciding whether to stop a lesson and focus the class's attention on the issue will depend upon a combination of factors: the age, awareness and sensitivity of the class, what work had already been done, the teacher's own style, and so on. This is where considering both short term and long-term responses is useful, since whatever one does on the spot usually feels inadequate; there is often a feeling that something more is needed. Planning for doing more later counters feelings of being overwhelmed or inadequate.

Deal appropriately with the offender. What would count as an appropriate response will vary enormously, but a rule that applies throughout is to develop consistency across the school.

Record and report the incident. This is obligatory. All schools should have a means of doing this, and brief details of incidents have to be reported to the LEA and governors once a year. LEA's aggregated returns have to be anonymised, but some teachers or schools may think they should aim at a nil return. Clearly it should be a goal to have no racist incidents, but a nil return might mean staff have not thought things through and do not take incidents seriously. It can also mean that pupils see no point in reporting them. A record of incidents can show the school is doing something, a nil return can show its eyes are closed.

The ways in which the recording might be done can be off-puttingly cumbersome and time-consuming. Standard forms in some LEAs run to several pages. With their usual weekly diet of form filling teachers may well groan at this, but the issue of racist incidents cannot be tackled without teachers recognising that such incidents vary and need recording in their variety so as to work effectively against them. On the matter of racist incident reporting paperwork, police officers have led the way. They have found that standardised forms are desirable across public bodies in specific areas, that the range of detail is necessary in order to spot patterns, and that joined-up action might then be taken. Take the example of an increasing amount of graffiti on a particular house with various clues that it was done by school children. For a typical form see page 122.

Whether or not there is an integrated public sector form, it is good practice to comply with the legal obligation to record incidents. In schools that keep a book logging bad behaviour, pupils know that racist behaviour will be logged. Schools need a concise and focused form, and teachers should practise using it in a CPD session working on one of the examples suggested. Filling in the form takes only a few minutes and demonstrating this undermines the complaint about oppressive paperwork.

Share and discuss with colleagues, because you won't be the only one to wonder about the many different ways you might respond. Professional knowledge grows this way. A book logging incidents will help produce a concerted approach.

INCIDENT REPORT FORM	ETHNICITY	GENDER	AGE	POSITION/ STATUS/ RELATIONSHIP TO SCHOOL
NAMES OF PERPETRATORS (IF KNOWN)				
NAME/S OF VICTIMS (IF ANY)				
NAME/S OF WITNESS/ES				
NAME/S OF PERSON/PEOPLE REPORTING				
'AUDIENCE' (IF ANY)				
LOCATION			TIME	

TYPE OF INCIDENT

'joke'	damaging belongings	threat	incitement/ racist materials/ badges	graffiti
derogatory stereotype/ comment in discussion	text/phone/ email	physical	explicit insult	other
ridicule	refusal to cooperate or work with			

PRELIMINARY JUDGEMENT OF

intention	gravity	frequency	other

Consider the school policy and guidelines. You might not have felt you needed to look at them before! Such consideration is likely to be a longer-term response, though a specific incident is the most likely catalyst to finding out what the guidelines actually say. Considering

other incidents will raise different questions about the policy or identify gaps – for instance, is there a specified time by which racist
graffiti, once reported, must be removed? How easy is it to report
incidents? In the light of the requirements of the law, schools should
have racist behaviour identified specifically in home-school agreements so that when parents of a perpetrator are contacted nego-
tiation or dispute is minimal. In one school cited by Cline *et al* it was
their policy to get offending pupils to write out a 'thinking sheet'
setting out why they were wrong. The pupil and parent have to sign
this, though the head remarked

> ... the parent has to sign to say they've seen it – they don't have to
> do anything – they just have to acknowledge that they've seen that
> their child has done something we're not happy about, but I must say
> that on 50 per cent of occasions when we've sent home instances of
> inappropriate behaviour towards ethnic minorities, we've had notes
> back saying 'I don't think he's done anything wrong'. (2002: 83)

Incidents involving adults

These are harder to deal with, so might be presented at a repeat
session a year after the first one focusing upon pupils. Especially difficult are those in the scenarios suggested which involve staff. In a
small primary school or a department setting in a secondary school
this may be so uncomfortable they do not get off the ground because
of a wave of denial.

A colleague makes an off the cuff 'joke' about black men having
bigger penises.

A minority ethnic student teacher confides to you that s/he feels
discriminated against by a colleague.

A male student teacher of Caribbean descent for whom you are
the professional tutor in school tells you he thinks he's going to
be accused of sexual harassment by a white female student. He's
convinced it's just because he's black.

Spoken by a parent with reference to the parking space of the
school's sole Asian member of staff: 'Oh, so that's where Ali parks
his camel is it?'

'My daughter's thinking of going to uni in Leicester. I told her to
take her passport to the interview'.

Said to a visiting member of a peripatetic service: 'When you started here I didn't think you would be any good at the job. But you've done ok so far!'

'I don't know about all this racism stuff. We lived in Hong Kong for a while and never had any problems. I just love the Orientals'.

'That little Angela can't half dance – she's certainly got the rhythm of her race'.

'I'm never sure about going for an Indian – you just don't know what goes on in the kitchen are you?'

'You just wouldn't know James was black really, would you, but then both his parents are professionals you know.'

A member of support staff 'whitens up' the face of a black child appearing as an angel in a nativity play. This really happened, in 2001, in a rural county in the south west.

In principle these scenarios can be explored in exactly the same way as the incidents involving pupils, and doing so would be powerful evidence that the school took race equality seriously. Again, they are likely to fuel the cyclical development of awareness and the real embedding of a policy.

Outcomes from this exercise should be considered in relation to the matrix and the suggested cycle at the end of Chapter 3. It should both raise general awareness and inform policy development. It might also cause some reorientation on the matrix of antiracist/anti-prejudice/hostile/indifferent I suggested in the same chapter.

Further guidance

Many LEAs have guidance about racial incidents. Two good ones are:
www.leicester.gov.uk/departments/page.asp?pgid=4406
www.blss.portsmouth.sch.uk/rra.shtml
A handbook for school and teacher development that deals with incidents thoroughly is *Here, There and Everywhere* by Robin Richardson (details in the resources chapter).

Note

1 I discuss the different contexts in which words might and might not be deemed offensive in Chapter 4. In brief, it seems to me unwise for any teacher in a mainly white school to condone the use of words like 'nigger' and 'paki' on the grounds that they seem to have some acceptance among young people themselves. It's too complicated to let it become part of school language and far better to get the pupils to analyse language and its power themselves.

6

What to do: Resources

A starting point

As a shameless piece of advertising – although I make no money from it – this chapter opens with mention of *Britkid*, the antiracist website for teenagers that I developed with Comic Relief's backing in the late 1990s. It is still on line at www.brit kid.org. In many ways it represents what I first argued for in the 1980s: an accessible resource for young people, aimed principally at white areas, dealing with diversity and cultural difference but also explicitly with racism and racist ideas. I have been surprised at how much it is used and liked by minority young people in the mixed areas that were not my original target, but also how many adults use it as an accessible and quickly digestible source of facts and arguments, some ways of seeing. It's free, it's user friendly for pupils and teachers, and it's authoritative, so it feels like a practical gift to give to all those teachers I have been urging over the years to tackle racism. I expect to update it during 2006, and it will be joined early that year by something in similar format but aimed at adults, principally student teachers. It also has sibling sites about the Netherlands, Spain, Sweden and the Czech Republic, all accessible in English through www.eurokid.org.

Where to go next

There are many conventional books and other resources in this list, though I have concentrated just as much on where to get both materials and information. Clearly many of us now rely upon the Internet for readily accessible information and support, and this has transformed accessing the kinds of things we need for antiracist development. I would need to be a human *Google* and this book the size of a phone-directory to include all that is available today, so I have included some information and curriculum sites but focused more on what seem like good portal sites which have done some of the sifting for you.

Materials useable by or with pupils

This section has to be limited somehow or it would cover everything from first readers, to novels for young people set in Africa, to sociology texts. Many of the former can be found in the publishers' lists referred to below. I have concentrated here on resources that focus more on racism than on diversity, on useable classroom materials, and featured resources that may not be widely known.

Bullying, name-calling

This is a vast topic which has seen a mushrooming of resources and websites in recent years. All the major sites (Childline; National Children's Bureau; Kidscape; BullyingonLine; Beatbullying; BBClic and Coastkid) have sections about racist bullying, though almost none are well designed for younger people in terms of font size, amount of information on the page and layout. The last two listed are exceptions.

Author/source	Title	Contact details (assume www)	KS	Comment
Anti Bullying Network (Scottish Executive)	*AntiBullying*	antibullying.net		Aimed at teachers, some advice and resources listed
Beatbullying	*Beatbullying*	bbclic.com	2/3/4	Go straight to www.bbclic.com/intro.html or you'll get lost. Racist bullying is covered in the basement. This is a well funded site that keeps developing and has lots of young involvement
Bullying on line	*Racist bullying*	Bullying.co.uk	3 and 4	Detailed and supportive comments and advice, with links elsewhere
Childline	*Racism*	Childline.org.uk	2/3/4	Detailed and supportive comments and advice, with links elsewhere
Gaine, C. /Brighton and Hove LEA	*Coastkid*	Coastkid.org	3/4	Scenarios and characters that explore bullying, specific pages on racist bullying and offensive terminology
Kidscape	*Preventing Racist Bullying, what schools can do*	Kidscape.org.uk	2/3/4	Detailed and supportive comments and advice, with links elsewhere

Teaching materials dealing with racism in Britain (for racism in other societies see the publishers and bookshops section). I have taken this focus because the bookshops and suppliers listed have stocks of many more titles dealing with diversity and culture. There are fewer materials and books that deal explicitly with racism (though these suppliers also stock these titles).

Author/source	Title	Contact details (assume www)	KS	Comment
Gaine, C. (2001)	*britkid*	University College Chichester/Comic Relief britkid.org	2/3/4	Very large site exploring racism and diversity through characterisation and narrative rather than description. Easy reading, attractive graphics
East Sussex LEA (2004)	One of Us	01273 293530	4	CD or video, interviews with young minorities in the county. Well made, clear and effective. Booklet with lesson ideas.
Every Generation	*100 Great Black Britons*	100greatblackbritons.com	3/4	Accessible and clearly signposted, photos and brief biogs of current and historic figures
Hampshire LEA (2004)	*Coming Unstuck: teaching about race and racism with 10-11 year olds*	HIAS Winchester Local Office Clarendon House Romsey Road Winchester SO22 5PW 01962 876264	3	Well thought out, comprehensive citizenship programme
Hoggan, J, Sewell, T. (2000)	*Off Limits – Teachers Guide: Talking About Race, Talking About Violence*	http://web.channel4.com/learning/main/netnotes//programid1197.htm	3/4	Channel 4 programme made for school use and with a teacher's guide. Will apparently be shown regularly

Author/source	Title	Contact details (assume www)	KS	Comment
Institute of Race Relations	*IRR News: independent race and refugees news network*	irr.org.uk	3 and 4	Critical/radical take on racism, many different sections
Institute of Race Relations (1999)	*Homebeats*	irr.org.uk info@irr.org.uk 020 7837 0041	4	CR Rom covering history of struggle for racial justice, connecting slavery, colonial experience, modern day racism. Stories of eight locations in Britain: Birmingham, Bradford, Brixton, East End, Glasgow, Liverpool, Notting Hill and Southall
Positive Images	Posters	Positive Images 36 Ermine Road Lewisham, SE13 7JS multicultural-art.co.uk	all	30 well-produced posters for class use and display, all visible on website
Runnymede Trust (2005)	*This is Where I Live*	Runnymede Trust	3/4	A CD made with young people in several locations around Britain showing the diversity and complexity of identity, with teaching suggestions
Rural Media Company	*Cyberace: Can You Beat Racism?*	ruralmedia.co.uk 01432 344039 Hereford: Rural Media Company	3	CD Rom meant for classroom use with a group or individuals, specifically with rural areas in mind. Includes definitions, video clips, interactive elements and some teacher notes, in a format many will find engaging

Books dealing with racism in Britain all purchasable from one or other of the bookshops and suppliers listed later

Thomas, P. (2004)	*The Skin I'm In*	1/2	London: Hodder Wayland
Bingham, J. (2005)	*Racism and Prejudice: Why Is It Wrong?*	3/4	London: Heinemann
Bradman, T. (ed) (2004)	*Skin Deep, a Collection of Stories About Racism*	2/3/4	London: Puffin
Cooper, A. (2003)	*Just the Facts: Racism*	3/4	London: Heinemann
Damon, E. (1995)	*All Kinds of People*	1	London: Tango Books
Edwards, N. (2005)	*Talking about Racism*	1/2	London: Chrysalis Children's Books
Gifford, C (2003)	*World Issues: Racism*	3/4	London: Chrysalis Children's Books
Green, J. (1999)	*Talking About Racism*	1/2	Oxford: Raintree
Green, J. (2002)	*What Do We Think About Racism*	1/2	London: Hodder Wayland
Gundara, J (1999)	*Racism (Life Files)*	2/3	London: Evans Brothers
Hibbert, A. (2003)	*In the News: the far right and racism*	3/4	London: Franklin Watts
Hibbert, A. (2004)	*Read All About It: Racism*	3/4	London: Franklin Watts
Donnellan, C. (2003)	*The Racism Debate*	3/4	Independence
Maddocks, S. (2004)	*Just the Facts: Refugees*	3/4	London: Heinemann
Neustatter, A. (2002)	*It Happened To Me: Refugee*	3/4	London: Franklin Watts
Sanders, B (2003)	*Talking About Racism*	1/2	London: Franklin Watts
Sanders, P. (2000)	*What Do You Know About Racism?*	2	London: Franklin Watts
Senker, C. (2002)	*Why are people racist?*	2/3	London: Hodder Wayland
Teichmann (2002)	*In the News: Immigration and Asylum*	3/4	Oxford: OUP
Wignall P. (2002)	*What's at Issue? Multicultural Britain*	3/4	London: Heinemann
Wignall P. (2002)	*What's at Issue? Prejudice and Difference*	3/4	London: Heinemann
Noah, I. (2003)	*Being Black: A Little Black Book of Pride and Prejudice*	3/4	London: Intermedia Press

Teachers' Materials

Really practical handbooks and guides. The main criterion for this section is that the resource must contain useable lesson plans!

Author/source	Title	Publisher/contact details (assume www)	KS	Comment
Anti-bullying network	Information about racist bullying	antibullying.net	2/3/4	Brief but sensible groundrules
Brown, B. (2001)	Combating Discrimination: Persona Dolls In Action	Stoke on Trent: Trentham Books	1	See 'Persona Doll Training' in CPD section
Brown, C., Barnfield, J. and Stone, M. (1990)	Spanner in the Works (Education for racial equality and social justice in white schools)	Stoke on Trent: Trentham Books	1 and 2	Detailed examples of good ideas and good practice from Cumbria primary schools. Out of print but worth seeking out in an education library.
Dadzie, S. (2000)	Toolkit for Tackling Racism in schools	Stoke on Trent: Trentham Books	3 and 4	Mainly a toolkit for staff to work on school development, with many useful prompts and activities. A few lesson ideas for secondary schools
Department for Education and Skills	Standards Site	standards.dfes.gov.uk/schemes3/ Use dialogue box for subject options and go to Citizenship	1/2/3/4	A few lesson plans in each key stage. www.dfes.gov.uk/citizenship/ brings you to the same place

Author/source	Title	Publisher/contact details (assume www)	KS	Comment
Friedman, E. (2002)	Making a Difference	London: Jewish Council for Racial Equality	3 and 4	Resources and lesson ideas and materials for secondary schools. Well suited to mainly white areas
Friedman, E., Woolfson, H., Freedman, S. and Murgraff, S. (1999)	Let's Make a Difference	London: Jewish Council for Racial Equality	1 and 2	Useable in any school, mostly well designed copyable pages with information and questions/exercises, some need more thought/elaboration
Gearon, L. (2003)	The Human Rights Handbook: a global perspective for education	Stoke on Trent: Trentham Books	3/4	Chapters on genocide, slavery, religion and belief, indigenous people, asylum and others
Klein, R. (2001)	Citizens by Right: citizenship education in primary schools	Stoke on Trent: Trentham Books	1 and 2	Makes citizenship relevant to young children and provides classroom activities
Knowles, E. and Ridley, W. (2005)	Another Spanner in the Works: challenging prejudice and racism in mainly white schools	Stoke on Trent: Trentham Books	2/3	Successor to Brown and Barnfield's excellent book
Multiverse (2004-on)	Multiverse: Exploring Diversity and Achievement	multiverse.ac.uk/ viewArticle.aspx?contentId=10752 (on Kindertransport)	all	TTA funded as a support for teachers. Large and growing, with lesson plans, this is just one example

Author/source	Title	Publisher/contact details (assume www)	KS	Comment
Qualifications and Curriculum Authority	*Respect for All* section of website	qca.org.uk/8859.html	1/2/3/4	Lesson plans with reflections on improvements, for every key stage and subject, written by teachers and being added to constantly. All lesson plans are linked to the appropriate NC bits and begins with the question 'what is the potential in the [subject] curriculum for valuing diversity and challenging racism?' Not all the ideas are self-evidently good, so need to be approached critically
Richardson, R. (2004)	*Here, There and Everywhere: Belonging, Identity and Equality in Schools*	Stoke on Trent: Trentham Books	3/4	Drawing extensively on work done in Derbyshire and compiled on their behalf. It asks big curriculum questions, has 46 pages of ideas an suggestions for every subject, useful material about ethos and relationships, and more
Runnymede Trust (2003)	*Complementing Teachers: a Practical Guide to Promoting Race Equality in Schools*	London: Granada Learning	all	Updates and builds upon Equality Assurance (1993). Sections on school leadership/ governance; teaching and learning strategies and key stages. Lesson plans for every subject and every key stage, with everything on CD too

Author/source	Title	Publisher/contact details (assume www)	KS	Comment
Rural Media Company (2000)	*Traveller Education In Wales*	Hereford: Rural Media Company	3/4	A ten minute video presented by Travellers, dealing with barriers to progress as well as celebrating some successes
Shan, S. and Bailey, P. (1991)	*Multiple Factors: mathematics for equality and social justice*	Stoke on Trent: Trentham Books	2/3/4	Very knowledgeable and practical. Expands the horizons of mathematics
St Martin's College	*Religious Education Exchange Service*	re-xs.ucsm.ac.uk	1/2/3/4	Large and comprehensive resource with detailed background material, lessons plans, policy stuff, routes to lots of specific faith websites
Supple, C. (1993, 3rd ed. 2005)	*From Prejudice to Genocide*	Stoke on Trent: Trentham Books	4	Highly detailed, packed with information and lesson guides
Thorp, S., Deshpande, P. and Edwards, C. (Eds.) (1991)	*Race, Equality and Science Teaching: A Handbook for teachers and educators*	Hatfield: Association for Science Education	1/2/3/4	Well thought out and authoritative, with ideas, starting points, lesson plans

Author/source	Title	Publisher/contact details (assume www)	KS	Comment
Thorp, S., Deshpande, P. and Edwards, C. (Eds.)(1994)	Race, Equality and Science Teaching: a handbook for teachers and educators	Hatfield: Association for Science Education	3 and 4	Unique publication combining clear analysis and discussion with practical suggestions for promoting and addressing equality and justice in primary and secondary classrooms
Vine, P. (2004)	Challenging Racism Through Quality Circle Time	Trowbridge: Positive Press	1 and 2	Highly practical handbook of lesson plans from Foundation to yr 6, itemising skills, knowledge and attitudes
Young, M and Commins, E. (2002)	Global Citizenship: the handbook for primary teaching	Oxford: Oxfam/Cambridge: Chris Kington Publishing	1 and 2	Does what it says on the tin. Effectively makes links between racism in Britain and ideas and judgements about other societies, in ways that work in primary school lessons

Support materials for CPD and staff workshops

There's some overlap here with the list above, but the focus here is on ready-made handouts to use with staff rather than pupils, workshop outlines, clear case studies and examples

Author/source	Title	Publisher/contact details (assume www)	Comment
Commission for Racial Equality (2002)	*Code of Practice on the Duty to Promote Race Equality: A Guide for Schools.*	London: CRE cre.gov.uk downloadable	Authoritative guide on what schools have to do. There is a separate Guide for Scotland
Dadzie, S. (2000)	*Toolkit for Tackling Racism in Schools*	Stoke on Trent: Trentham Books	Mainly a toolkit for staff to work on school development, many useful prompts and activities. A few lesson ideas for secondary schools.
DfES (2002)	*Supporting pupils learning English as an additional language*	standards.dfes.gov.uk/literacy/ publications/inclusion/63381/	Focused guidance, including use of TAs, links to using home languages in literacy hour, isolated learners
DfES (2003)	*Aiming High: Raising the Achievement of Gypsy Traveller Pupils*	standards.dfes.gov.uk/ethnic minorities/links_and_publications/ (Ref DfES/0443/2003) also downloadable	Range of practical advice and guidance for schools on raising attainment and achievement. Brief outline of communities, identifies key factors that schools need to consider

Author/source	Title	Publisher/contact details (assume www)	Comment
DfES (2004)	Aiming High: Guidance on Supporting the Education of Asylum Seeking and Refugee Children	standards.dfes.gov.uk/ethnic minorities/links_and_publications/ (Ref DfES/0287/2004) also downloadable	Intended as useful guidance and support
DfES (2004)	Aiming High: Understanding the Educational Needs of Minority Ethnic Pupils in Mainly White Schools	standards.dfes.gov.uk/ethnic minorities/links_and_publications/ (ref DfES/0416/2004) also downloadable	Compiled by Robin Richardson, a true expert in this field. In 28 pages it packs in much accessible and actionable advice, and has the formal legitimacy of being a government publication
DfES (2004)	Research: Understanding the Needs of Mixed Heritage Pupils	standards.dfes.gov.uk/ethnic minorities/links_and_publications/ (ref DfES RR 549) also downloadable	Specific reference to the barriers to achievement faced by White/black Caribbean pupils (though sample is from schools with 10% or more minority ethnic pupils).
DFID, DfES, QCA, DEA, British Council.	Developing the Global Dimension in the School Curriculum	Free from dept for International Development: 0845 300 4100. Also downloadable dea.org.uk/schools/publications.html	Shows how the global dimension can be integrated into both the curriculum and the wider life of schools. Includes subject-by-subject guide and NC links. Case studies, classroom and whole-school activities.
Elliot, Jane (1969 and 1975)	The Eye of the Storm; A Class Divided	Concordvideo.co.uk (to buy or hire)	Stunning films of classroom experiment in racism. The second one contains most of the first plus good extra material, never fails to engage and provoke discussion

Author/source	Title	Publisher/contact details (assume www)	Comment
Jones, C. and Rutter, J. (1998)	*Refugee Education: mapping the field*	Stoke on Trent: Trentham Books	Examples of good practice in secondary schools
Learning and Teaching Scotland (2002)	*Educating for Race Equality: a Toolkit for Scottish Teachers*	antiracisttoolkit.org.uk ltscotland.org.uk/edresources/ software.asp (then 'whole school')	With potential for further growth, this has some useful case studies and ideas. Also available as a much more detailed CD, with CPD exercises, printable handouts
Learning and Teaching Scotland (2003)	*Inclusive Educational Approaches for Gypsies and Travellers*	ltscotland.org.uk/resources/travellers. pdf	Full and detailed info and guidance, well presented. Downloadable and useable free in Scotland
Leung, C. and South, H. (Eds) (2001)	*Teaching English as an Additional Language in the Mainstream Curriculum: Vignettes of Classroom Practice*	National Association for Language Development in the Curriculum (main focus is EAL) naldic.org.uk	Just as in the title, useful and realisable models in the case studies. The website has downloadable lesson ideas
National Association of Head Teachers (2005)	*Primary Leadership Paper 14: Race Equality and Multicultural education*	London: NAHT	Brief and highly focused sections on the legal and policy framework of what schools have to do, followed by case studies, many in white areas. Also covers Travellers and refugees
Pavilion Publishing (1993)	*Training for Equality*	Harlow: Longman	A training manual to use with colleagues, with a variety of options built in for different starting points and foci

Author/source	Title	Publisher/contact details (assume www)	Comment
Persona Doll Training (undated)	*Persona Dolls in Action*	London: Persona Doll Training	A 50 minute video and support book (sold together) that give an accessible guide to this non-threatening early years approach
Richardson, R. (2004)	*Here, There and Everywhere: Belonging, Identity and Equality in Schools*	Stoke on Trent: Trentham Books	Drawing extensively on work done in Derbyshire and compiled on their behalf. It asks big curriculum questions, has 46 pages of ideas as suggestions for every subject, useful material about ethos and relationships, and more
Runnymede Trust (1993)	*Equality Assurance*	London: Runnymede Trust	Covers all areas of school life as well as all curriculum areas, summarises what good practice would look like. But see *Complementing Teachers* in the previous section, which updates and largely replaces it
Thorp, S. (Ed.) (1991)	*Race, Equality and Science Teaching: An active inset manual for teachers and educators*	Hatfield: Association for Science Education	Rooted in the classroom, and looks through good curriculum practice based on wide experience of the ASE Multicultural Working Party
Tyler, C. (2005)	*Traveller Education: accounts of good practice*	Stoke on Trent: Trentham Books	Many experienced contributors, dwells on positive strategies

Digestible and accessible sources for teachers. These may need teacher editing and planning

Author/source	Title	Publisher/contact details (assume www)	KS	Comment
BBC	BBC News: Race UK	news.bbc.co.uk/hi/english/static/in_depth/uk/2002/race/default.stm (not www)	all	Many pages of brief and focused information
Elliot, Jane (1969 and 1975)	The Eye of the Storm; A Class Divided	Concordvideo.co.uk (to buy or hire)	2/3/4	Stunning films of classroom experiment in racism. The second one contains most of the first plus very good extra material
Every Generation	100 Great Black Britons	100greatblackbritons.com	all	Accessible and clearly signposted, photos and brief biographies of current and historic figures
Gaine, C (1999)	britkid.org	University College Chichester/Comic Relief britkid.org	2/3/4	Aimed at lower secondary age pupils, but a mine of information useful to teachers
Muslim Association of Britain	mabonline	mabonline.info/English/	3/4	News, views, commentary, good search facility
Muslim Council of Britain	MCB	mcb.org.uk	3/4	As above, also good library, factsheets etc
Institute of Race Relations	IRR News: independent race and refugees news network	irr.org.uk	3/4	Critical/radical take on racism, many different sections

Author/source	Title	Publisher/contact details (assume www)	KS	Comment
Multiverse (2004-on)	*Multiverse: Exploring Diversity and Achievement*	multiverse.ac.uk (based at London Metropolitan University)	all	An Initial Teacher Training Professional Resource Network (IPRN) backed by the TTA. Large and growing, it has everything from ethnic breakdowns of specific LEAs to recent news. Search for 'white areas' and it gives 65 items, including article abstracts
Portsmouth Ethnic Minority Achievement Service	*Portsmouth EMAS*	blss.portsmouth.sch.uk	all	Absolute gold mine of school management tools, classroom resources, regularly updated amazing language facts, specific sections on early years, refugees, SEN, pupil case studies and more
Qualifications and Curriculum Authority	*Pathways to learning for new arrivals*	qca.org.uk/8476.html	all	General guidance, some background on different groups, specific curriculum guidance, almost gets to lesson plans but not quite
Scottish Executive	*One Scotland*	onescotland.com	all	Range of specific Scottish info that can otherwise be hard to find: personal stories emailed to the site; useful contacts in Scotland; explanations and dates for main religious festivals; facts about and experiences of Travellers, refugees; opinion surveys

Author/source	Title	Publisher/contact details (assume www)	KS	Comment
Wood, A and Richardson, R. (1993)	*Inside Stories*	Stoke on Trent: Trentham Books	2/3/4	An inspiring and imaginative text for assemblies and class
Sikhkids	*sikhkids*	sikhkids.com	2/3/4	A British site, ...'to give young Sikh people support and the platform to share their views experiences and knowledge with each other'
Refugee Council		refugeecouncil.org.uk	all	For a wide range of information and resources on refugees and asylum-seekers
BBC	*United Colours of London*	bbc.co.uk/londonlive. Click on the icon for United Colours of London	all	Basic facts about ten separate communities: Bangladeshi, Caribbean, Chinese, Ethiopian, Greek, Indian, Irish, Pakistani, Turkish and West African. Focus is on London, but most of the information is relevant for the whole of Britain.
Black History Month	*Black History Month*	black-history-month.co.uk	all	Held in October each year, the site is always present but fills up with news as the month approaches.
Willesden Bookshop	*Refugees, Migrations, Escaping Persecution*	See publishers and book shop section	all	Whole section of books (mostly stories) on these topics

Advisory/CPD texts about race and education not necessarily written with white areas in mind but with some links

Author/source	Title	Publisher	Comment
Alladina, S (1995)	*Being Bilingual: A Guide for Parents, teachers and young people*	Stoke on Trent: Trentham Books	Now out of print, but authoritative and accessible. Very useful if you are new to bilingual learners
Brown, B. (1998)	*Unlearning Discrimination in the Early Years*	Stoke on Trent: Trentham Books	Challenges preconceptions about early childhood development – e.g. that children cannot understand issues to do with fairness, or with skin colour or disability or homophobia. Explains relevant theory and research, and gives examples of good practice
Centre for Multicultural Education, London University Institute of Education 1993	*Sagaland*	Centre for Multicultural Education, London University Institute of Education	Research and reflection on the construction of hardened racist beliefs in working class youths in SE London, commissioned by Greenwich LEA. Very useful insights about how some young people make sense of their world. Probably only available now in libraries
Claire, H. (1996)	*Reclaiming our Pasts: Equality and Diversity in the Primary History Curriculum*	Stoke on Trent: Trentham Books	Very thorough, packed with useable information, examples and ideas

Author/source	Title	Publisher	Comment
Commission for Racial Equality (2000)	Learning for All: Standards for Racial Equality in Schools	London: CRE	Sets out what schools ought to be doing in all areas of their work, though it just preceded Race Relations Amendment Act, which increased schools' legal duties. Auditing checklists supplied on disk.
Commission for Racial Equality (2002)	Code of Practice on the Duty to Promote Race Equality: A Guide for Schools.	London: CRE Downloadable: cre.gov.uk	Authoritative guide on what schools have to do. There is a separate Guide for Scotland
Derrington, C. and Kendall, S. (2004)	Gypsy Traveller Students in Secondary Schools: culture, identity and achievement	Stoke on Trent: Trentham Books	Unique research study providing guidance on effective support of Gypsy Travellers in secondary schools
Education Leeds (2004)	Promoting Race Equality in Schools	Leeds: Education Leeds	Practical guidance and case studies for Leeds schools, but lots of useful stuff for elsewhere
Gaine, C and George, R (1999)	Gender, 'Race,' Class and Schooling	London: Falmer	The section on race covers key debates briefly and accessibly
Hill, D and Cole, M. (2001)	Schooling and Equality	London: Kogan Page	Not a practical handbook, but aimed at teachers who want to think and act about the social and political context of inequality in schools
Issa, T. (2005)	Talking Turkey: the language, culture and identity of Turkish speaking children in Britain	Stoke on Trent: Trentham Books	Useful background information on a little researched group

Author/source	Title	Publisher	Comment
Jones, R (1999)	*Tackling Racism, or Teaching it?*	Stoke on Trent: Trentham Books	Well written research study of the experiences of white trainees in mainly white schools, challenging to complacency and liberal good intentions. Out of print
Multiverse (2004-on)	*Multiverse: Exploring Diversity and Achievement*	multiverse.ac.uk (based at London Metropolitan University)	Initial Teacher Training Professional Resource Network (IPRN) backed by the TTA. Large and growing, it has everything from ethnic breakdowns of specific LEAs to recent news. Search for 'white areas' and it gives 65 items, including article abstracts
Naidoo, B (1992)	*Through Whose Eyes?*	Stoke on Trent: Trentham Books	Still useful account of exploring racism through literature with year 9 pupils
Osler, A. (Ed) 2005	*Teachers, Human Rights and Diversity: educating citizens in multicultural democracies*	Stoke on Trent: Trentham Books	Recent case studies from England, Ireland and USA
Osler, A. and Vincent, K. (2002)	*Citizenship and the Challenge of Global Education*	Stoke on Trent: Trentham Books	Considers the integration of citizenship, human rights and multiculturalism, against backdrop of media and political messages
Parker-Jenkins M. (1995)	*Children of Islam*	Stoke on Trent: Trentham Books	Readable and clear, useful for anyone uncertain about and supporting Muslim pupils
Peters, W (1987)	*A Class Divided*	London and New Haven: Yale University Press	Brief but fascinating written account of the famous blue eyes/brown eyes experiment (see Elliot)

Author/source	Title	Publisher	Comment
Trentham Books	Race Equality Teaching	Stoke on Trent: Trentham Books	3 times a year journal, shortish articles, focused on professional practice, almost always something relevant to white areas
Richardson, R (2004)	Here, There and Everywhere: belonging, identity and equality in schools	Stoke on Trent: Trentham Books	Partly about a rural secondary school linking and communication with a mixed urban school. Relates to every curriculum area
Rutter, J. (2003)	Supporting Refugee Children in 21st Century Britain	Stoke on Trent: Trentham Books	Comprehensive, authoritative, practical
Siraj-Blatchford, I. (1994)	The Early Years: laying the foundations for racial equality	Stoke on Trent: Trentham Books	The fact that it's been reprinted several times testifies to its continuing relevance and usefulness.
Siraj-Blatchford, I., Clarke, C. (2000)	Supporting Identity, Diversity and Language in the Early Years	Buckingham: Open University	Readable clear and focused
Tomlinson, S. (1990)	Multicultural Education in White Schools	London: Batsford	Very readable account of how we got to where we are today
Tyler, C. (Ed) (2005)	Traveller Education: accounts of good practice	Stoke on Trent: Trentham Books	Chapters cover many regions and all sectors from preschool to post 16
van Driel, B. (2004)	Confronting Islamophobia in Educational Practice	Stoke on Trent: Trentham Books	Unusual in that it gives several different European comparisons, while aiming at being really useful for teachers in devising their own approach

Good publishers and suppliers

Their entire catalogues would fill another book. Almost all have good informational websites that show you each book and tell you something about it. Though it has to be a good idea to support these specialist outfits, it's also worth remembering that if you key one relevant title into Amazon.co.uk, the site will tell you about possibly dozens of other books bought by people who bought the one you know. Opt for 'Fiction dealing with multiculturalism' and Amazon will show you over 500 titles (which you don't have to buy from them).

Name	Address	Web (assume www)	Main products and comments
Alpha Education	PO Box 6655 Nottingham, NG5 9BU 0115 976 2821 alphaedu@aol.com	alphaeducation.co.uk	Large stock
Articles Of Faith	Resource House, Kay Street, Bury BL9 6BU	articlesoffaith.co.uk	Religious artefacts and resources by mail order
DIVA Training and Consultancy	contact Patgreenpurple@hotmail.com (Oxford)	None yet, but contact Patgreenpurple@hotmail.com	Books, posters, videos with a special emphasis on black history
Frances Lincoln (includes Tamarind)	4 Torriano Mews Torriano Avenue London, NW5 2RZ	Franceslincoln.com (then click 'browse')	Excellent KS1 and 2
Kent National Grid for Learning	See website	kented.org.uk/ngfl/subjects/literacy/traveller/	Good list to support the use of Traveller culture in the Literacy Hour, many from other Traveller Ed Services
Letterbox Library	71-73 Allen Road, Stoke Newington, London N16 8RY	Letterboxlibrary.com	Non-profit workers co-operative. started 18 years ago by two single mothers operating from home, to provide multicultural and non-sexist books for children – offering essential topics and titles neglected by mainstream booksellers. Go for the list entitled 'Celebrating Equality and Diversity'

Name	Address	Web (assume www/)	Main products and comments
Lucky Duck	luckyduck.co.uk/contact/	luckyduck.co.uk	Not huge stock on race issues, but very well conceived classroom stuff, excellent on bullying, and some specific books to support asylum seekers
Mantra	Global House 303 Ballards Lane London, N12 8NP	Mantralingua.com	Bilingual children's books, CDs and friezes
Multicultural Books formerly Paublo Books	See website	multiculturalbooks.co.uk	Not a huge stock, but some unusual and carefully selected titles, well worth a browse
Multicultural Book Services	Unit 3 Carlisle Business Centre 60 Carlisle Road Bradford BD8 8BD 01274 544158	aamirdarr@multicultural bookservice.fsnet.co.uk	None yet but imminent in early 2005 Large stock, separate lists by age group. Particularly good for dual language books
Norfolk Traveller Education	Norfolk Traveller Education Service	www.norfolkesinet.org.uk	Various pop up books, videos, posters and a play trailer with furniture. F/KS1
Positive Identity	P.O. Box 17709, London, SE6 4ZQ	Positiveidentity.com	Multicultural toys, dolls, books
Raga-Muffins	148 Evington Lane Evington Leicester LE5 6DG	tutor-direct.co.uk	Unusual and excellent collection of hard to find texts for all ages. Poetry, a world perspective on Tudors and Stuarts, picture books for the early years: it's all here.

Name	Address	Web (assume www)	Main products and comments
Soma books	38 Kennington Lane, London SE11 4LS	childrens-books.uk.com	Wide of multicultural books for children, dual language material, titles on different faiths, cultures and traditions, antiracist and positive image titles, health and social issues and material helpful to teachers in these areas.
The Festival Shop	56 Poplar Road, Kings Heath, Birmingham B14 7AG	festivalshop.co.uk	Multifaith and citizenship resources
Trentham Books	Westview House, 734 London Road, Stoke on Trent, ST4 5NP	trentham-books.co.uk	Undoubtedly the best publishers for teachers on race equality. Mainly advisory but many practical manuals, listed in the other tables here
Willesden Bookshop	Willesden Green Library Centre, 95 High Road, London NW10 4QU 020-8451 7000 books@willesdenbookshop. co.uk	willesdenbookshop.co.uk.	The large stock leans more to the primary sector, and has some unusual and excellent books from the USA (and 27 versions of Cinderella!) KS 3/4 material is mostly fiction and biography.

7

Antiracist work in mainly white higher education

Introduction

This chapter explores some of the practical and conceptual dilemmas facing the higher education institutions (HEIs) in England where black and minority ethnic students are under-represented. Unlike schools, HEIs are not in any obvious way limited by catchment areas and thus in principle could have student bodies that differ demographically from their own immediate localities. Many of these localities are very white. To take some southern examples, the universities of Plymouth, Exeter, Bournemouth, Winchester, Chichester, Kent, Canterbury, Essex, Cambridge, East Anglia, Oxford and Gloucester are located in areas where the black and minority ethnic population is less than 4 per cent and in most cases larger populations are more than daily commuting distance away on student incomes. Even a city like Southampton only has a black and minority ethnic population of 7.6 per cent and Brighton's is only 5.5 per cent (ONS, 2005). In common with other public bodies, however, they are required by the Race Relations Amendment Act (RRRA) to address race equality, and this is generally taken to mean ensuring that institutional processes are not presenting barriers to higher minority recruitment. This analysis of higher education in general affects teacher education in particular, since virtually all HEIs have teacher education departments.

The complexity of 'racial' generalisations and the strategies needed in white areas to progress in an antiracist direction keeps increasing. There are two key themes: identifying the problem and devising a specific 'white areas' strategy. We need to be clear how we identify the problem, and we need strategies and approaches not directly inherited from mixed metropolitan settings.

The first theme is largely about unravelling the variations in informed choice, economic advantage, and educational success against the odds of the different black and minority ethnic groups. This is not an issue that can sensibly be discussed in 'black and white' terms. Nevertheless, data about groups is presented as counterposed with whites and then distinguished by ethnicity (Chinese, Pakistani etc). We are the prisoners of national data gathering categories: there is no useful data yet on the higher education trajectory of Travellers, the Irish, or newer eastern European migrants and data on the range of African circumstances and roots is still unsophisticated.

On the second theme, the statutory demands of the RRRA have brought together institutions – or the key players within them – who have little experience of race equality work, and 'Londocentric' agencies seeking to apply metropolitan perspectives and strategies inappropriately. So we need to think out what a sound 'white areas' strategy would be.

The complex challenge from the Race Relations Amendment Act

The RRAA presents mainly white HEIs with three challenges. The first, generally regarded as the primary one, is ensuring there are no institutional barriers to recruiting BME staff and students, so possibly recruiting more. The second and harder challenge is to consider the curriculum experienced by all students. The third is critically to examine the general experience to do with race equality of everyone at the institution.

They are linked in ways that should constantly inform each other. A curriculum that engages with race equality entails a teaching staff that is sensitive and reflective about the issue. The goal of such a curriculum would be a student body concerned about and aware of race in/equality. A positive general experience with regard to race equality entails support staff understanding and ownership of strategies about recruitment, monitoring, language use and wel-coming diversity. Together, these things would contribute towards making an institution more attractive to black and minority ethnic students and staff.

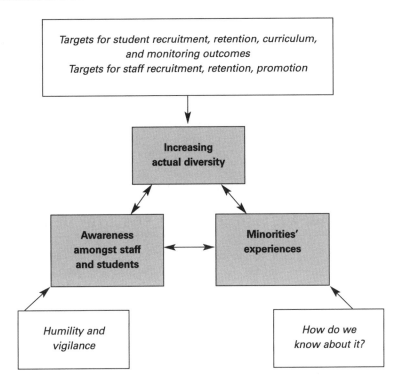

Many HEIs need to be realistic about recruitment aims and put at least as much effort into the second two challenges, since the first has some inherent limitations. This is based upon the following proposi-tions:

■ Minority ethnic groups are not under-represented nationally in HE[1]

■ BME students have clear subject preferences which not all institutions can match, especially the smaller ones

■ Less prestigious institutions recruit largely from the surrounding counties and are unlikely to draw students from further afield

■ In such areas the local pool of black and minority ethnic people qualified and potentially interested in HE is demonstrably small

■ BME students' current concentration in a small number of institutions is likely to be heavily influenced by *informed* choice, that is to say they are not necessarily there by default or because other institutions have rejected them – though sometimes they are.

The national pool of black and minority ethnic students

We need first to be clear about numbers: national, local, by age co-hort and by ethnic group. General statements derived from the Census, such as that 7.9 per cent of the population are from a non-white ethnic group, are not very useful since they obscure the fact that the proportion is lower amongst older people and higher amongst the young.

This table is therefore more informative for our purposes:

PERCENTAGE AGE DISTRIBUTION: BY ETHNIC GROUP, 2001/02

	Under 16	16-64	65 and over	All ages
White	19	65	16	92.1
Mixed	55	43	2	1.2
Indian	22	71	6	1.8
Pakistani	35	61	4	1.3
Bangladeshi	38	58	3	0.5
Other Asian	22	74	4	0.4
Black Caribbean	25	67	9	1.0
Black African	33	66	2	0.8
Other Black	35	60	5	0.2
Chinese	18	77	5	0.4
Other ethnic groups	20	76	4	0.4

The table illustrates how much the skewed age distribution varies be-tween different ethnic groups. Thirty eight per cent of Bangladeshis are under 16, twice as many as whites, and the difference is almost as great for Pakistanis and 'other black' people[2]. There are larger numbers of young 'mixed' people because mixed relationships are increasing: the table above shows 55 per cent are under 16, in fact 70 per cent are under 25 (Labour Force Survey, 2002).

So, whereas around 8 per cent of the entire population is from BME groups, for secondary school pupils the figure is 13.1 per cent. Extra-polating to 18 year olds, this suggests that overall around 13 per cent of first year HE students should be from BME groups.

Who gets to higher education?

Interestingly, the Higher Education Funding Council for England (HEFCE) figures suggest that the overall figure of UK resident, non-overseas students is higher than this at 17 per cent:

ETHNICITY OF UK DOMICILED FIRST YEAR STUDENTS IN ENGLISH HEIs

	2002-03	
Ethnicity	Headcount	% known ethnicity
White	514,395	83.1
Bangladeshi	3,825	0.6
Indian	23,580	3.8
Pakistani	12,790	2.1
Chinese	6,195	1.0
Other Asian background	8,885	1.4
African	19,105	3.1
Caribbean	10,250	1.7
Other Black background	3,560	0.6
Mixed – White and Asian	3,190	0.5
Mixed – White and Black African	1,415	0.2
Mixed – White and Black Caribbean	2,005	0.3
Other Mixed background	3,535	0.6
Other Ethnic background	6,515	1.1
Total known ethnicities	**619,250**	**100.0**
Information refused	35,085	
Not known	40,555	
Grand total	**694,890**	

HEFCE, 2005

Note that the ethnicity of 75,000 students, more than 10 per cent, is either not known or 'refused', so given other HEFCE data indicating that in 2000-1 13 per cent of HE students were from BME groups, it seems likely that most of the refusers in this table were white. This is a large number in relation to the total number of identified minority students, which is around 100,000. The effect of these white refusals is to make it more difficult to analyse and counter the effects of race. As a factor in people's lives race doesn't go away just because some white people deny its relevance in their own.

Nevertheless, these figures make it clear that there is not a straightforward pattern of under-representation. This is reinforced by a government statistical formula called the Higher Education Participation Rate (HEIPR), which is far more complex than the tables created above (it uses the sums of percentages participating between 17 and 30 years old). This shows an even greater disparity between white and BME entry into universities, indicating that in the 17-30 age group the white HEIPR is the lowest of all groups: only 38 per cent, compared with 71 per cent for Indians, 49 per cent for Chinese, and 45 per cent for Black Caribbeans (Home Office, 2005). A higher participation rate for Caribbean people than whites? How can this be?

18 year olds

Some of this is explained by age. The following table focuses on under- and over-representation. We know that groups achieve differentially at 16+ and 18+, key examination gateways for qualifying for entry into HE, so we would expect differential rates of entry to HEIs from school outcomes. This is explored in the table which combines some of the previous ones and shows percentages of BME groups in HE alongside their numbers in the age cohort and in the general population, together with school success rates.

These figures do not indicate significant under-representation of BME students; indeed only with the mixed White/Black Caribbean group is there a significant negative mismatch. Recent findings (Home Office, 2005) argue that BME people are as likely overall as whites to gain HEI entry qualifications by the age of 19, though – except for Indians and Chinese – at a lower level. So they must be generally more interested in going to university and a greater proportion do so.

Mature students

The issue of age clarifies matters further. More of the white students get to HE at 18, more of the BME students take longer and gain entry through access courses or other courses taken later, and this age factor varies widely between ethnic groups. Sometimes, therefore, like is not quite compared with like: a high proportion of the white students begin at around 18 years old, more of the BME students are older. This is not true for the Chinese, for instance, who are the most successful group in school, but one can see the effect of racial disadvantage delaying the entry into HE for some groups. Entry also

Ethnicity	% in general population	% of secondary pupils (2003)	Success rate grades A-C at GCSE (2002)	% of those in HE yr 1 for whom ethnicity known (2002)
White	92.1	86.9	52	83.1
Bangladeshi	0.5	1.0	45	0.6
Indian	1.8	2.5	65	3.8
Pakistani	1.3	2.4	41	2.1
Other Asian background	0.4	0.6	Not known	1.4
Chinese	0.4	0.4	74	1.0
African	0.8	1.4	38	3.1
Caribbean	1.0	1.5	33	1.7
Other Black background	2.1	0.4	30	0.6
Mixed White and Asian	1.2	0.4	Not known	0.5
Mixed White and Black African	1.2	0.2	Not known	0.2
Mixed White and Black Caribbean	1.2	0.7	Not known	0.3
Other Mixed background	1.2	0.7	Not known	0.6
Other Ethnic background	0.4	0.8	Not known	1.1
Total known ethnicities	7.9%	99.9%	Not known	100.0%

Sources: Census, April 2001, Office for National Statistics and Pupil Annual School Census (PLASC), 2003, DfES; HEFCE; Source: National Pupil Database (NPD) version 2, entered for GCSEs, having a PLASC record

varies with gender: in all groups except Bangladeshis and Pakistanis, women are more likely to go to higher education than men.

Ironically, the age factor has presented one institution with a specific practical limit to recruiting more BME students. As an institution it does well at recruiting mature students, those who for various reasons missed out on higher education when they were younger. Mature students made up over 30 per cent of the undergraduate intake in 2003-4, 24.7 per cent through access rather than traditional qualifications. But nationally most mature students study near where they already live: they are more likely than 18 year olds to have family and housing commitments that make them less mobile in their HEI choice. This is clearly the case with the institution in question's 850 mature students, virtually all of whom lived within a 40-mile radius which contains perhaps two per cent BME adults.

Determining factors for HE entry and choice

Younger students are in principle not restricted by geography in where they go for higher education. They will be influenced by four primary factors: qualifications, finance, subject preference and aspiration and perceptions of HE (both nationally and in relation to specific institutions).

Qualifications: different proportions of different groups are eligible for entry and take up HEI places. In general minority ethnic degree entrants have lower entry qualifications (Home Office, 2005: 32) but this is not true of Indian and Chinese applicants and by their early 20s almost all groups have more eligible candidates for HE than whites.

Finance is an issue whatever one's ethnicity, and it is noteworthy that the groups with the lowest take-up of HE places are also the least well off economically: African-Caribbeans, Pakistanis and Bangladeshis earn less than other minority ethnic groups and less than whites and are more likely to be unemployed (Home Office, 2005). Fifty per cent of Bangladeshi pupils receive free school meals, 42 per cent of Black Africans, 35 per cent of Pakistanis, compared with around 12 per cent of white, Indian and Chinese pupils. Class, then, cannot be ignored, though it may be masked by ethnicity to produce what looks like an 'ethnic effect'. We know that most BME groups are more likely to go to university in London and to the ex-polytechnics, and that students from poorer postcodes are more likely than better off students to choose HEIs nearer home.

But neither qualifications nor finance can be regarded as providing a comprehensive account for the relative absence of BME students at certain HEIs. We can gain some insight into *subject preference and aspiration* by looking at the subjects taken up by BME students. The next table shows the numbers (not percentages) of a selection of BME groups who took up undergraduate HE places in 2003 in specific subject categories in England and Wales:

FIRST YEAR STUDENTS, ENGLISH and WELSH HEIs, 2003, NUMBERS

	Caribbean	Indian	Pakistani	Bangladeshi	Chinese
Math and Comp Sciences	140	1709	1098	296	227
Medicine	14	691	271	65	129
Law	150	873	616	176	89
Business and Admin Studies	199	1947	834	278	289
Subjects Allied to Medicine	71	922	588	135	103
Social Studies	127	938	350	166	152
Biological Sciences	194	705	320	133	52
Creative Arts and Design	269	319	62	40	171
English	55	123	47	44	23
History	32	133	64	31	18
Mass Communications	133	205	61	36	39
Education	28	67	58	24	15

Source: UCAS

The figures are remarkably low in some subjects and remarkably high in others. So of the 23,580 Indians in their first year in HE, about 7,000 went into just four subjects. Of the 12,790 Pakistanis, over 3,500 went into business studies, mathematics, law, medicine and allied subjects. Some of this is choice and preference and some is not. It would be hard to believe that there were only fourteen – yes, fourteen – first year medical students of Caribbean descent because none want to be doctors. On the other hand, the presence of only fifteen Chinese students in undergraduate education courses probably reflects active preferences for other careers.

So BME students as a percentage of total student numbers by subject in English universities is as follows:

	PERCENTAGES
Computer science	38
Medicine and dentistry	35
Law	30
Business and administrative studies	25
Mathematical sciences	22
Engineering and technology	21
Subjects allied to medicine	19
Librarianship and information science	19
Social, economic and political science	19
Biological science	15
Architecture building and planning	13
Physical sciences	10
Creative arts and design	10
Languages	8
Education	6
Humanities	6
	SOURCE: UCAS

Looking at these national patterns there is clear evidence of an instrumental orientation. A class analysis shows this is true irrespective of class: there is no great difference in degree subject choice between those from white collar and manual homes. There might be some correlation between white middle class students having the cultural capital and economic security to take a subject with no clear career outcome and the freedom to make less instrumental degree choice. This speculative comparison is of limited use, however, since we do not know how many of the BME students, while coming from middle class families in occupational terms are nevertheless the first in their families to go to university. This is frequently the case with the most successful group of all, Indian students (Modood *et al*, 1997).

A case can be made that particular subjects are unpopular with BME students because of their content, that a Eurocentric curriculum can have a excluding effect, that history focusing upon Britain is un-attractive to those with roots elsewhere, that English literature focused upon the traditional canon reflects too little of the lives and heritages of minorities. This argument has been effectively related to school success and the alienation of some groups of pupils, but there are limits as to how much the argument is tenable for higher education. Firstly, subjects that might appear to reflect something of the culture and background of minorities do not attract many in national terms: most of those studying oriental languages, for instance, are white. Secondly, subject areas at some institutions that have made specific and detailed efforts to address this issue, for instance in geography, religious studies, history and English, have not recruited more BME students.

Thus a major limitation is the subject base of some institutions, especially smaller ones. In the case of one smallish institution, with the exception of a single newly launched Business Studies and IT degree, not a single one of its current courses is in a subject area that attracts significant numbers of BME students. Indeed there is almost an inverse correlation between popular BME choices nationally and the subjects it offers. A 'simple' answer to this might be to sack most of the current staff, offering as they are a curriculum that clearly appeals more to white people, and open new departments with a wider appeal. This does not seem like a financially plausible solution.

Perceptions of HE institutions, nationally and locally has two aspects: the academic status of an institution and how 'friendly' it and its locality appears to BME students, what is the racial ambiance?

Status is obviously a magnet. The fact that Cambridge was mainly white did not stop Gandhi, Nehru or Salman Rushdie from going there; the whiteness of Oxford did not stop Stuart Hall or many an African independence activist from valuing their time there. High status institutions in largely white localities may present contradictory images to minority students: on the one hand, highly prized and desirable, but on the other characterised by an exclusivity that could daily marginalise and exclude. If the gains are potentially high enough, there is clearly a trade-off many people would be prepared to make. But these are the extremes. For most HEIs and students things are not so clear-cut, and a complex deal has to be struck between different and perhaps competing goals, just as white students have to do. Where one wants to spend three or more formative and potentially exciting years is at least as important a calculation as course content and structure.

Racial ambiance

Little work has been done on the effect upon BME applicants of their perceptions of the 'climate' and atmosphere of institutions and their localities. It is quite a nebulous thing to measure, especially as it is about impressions (though see Givens and Bennett, 2004 and Cole and Stuart, 2005). Cambridge has a very different 'ethnic feel' to much of London, but a London-born black student who gets a place there may consider it worth it. Plymouth or Norwich may feel different again and offer a less definite payoff, and in the case of newer and lower status institutions the difficulties may be compounded. In two recent studies of non-university life in largely white south coast cities without particularly prestigious HEIs, we found pervasive attitudes and a range of experiences which generally came as an unpleasant shock to many minorities who had lived in more mixed areas (Gough and Gaine, 2000; Gaine and Lamley, 2003). Older and less detailed studies in Devon and Cornwall and in Norfolk reveal similar patterns. Potential students might reasonably expect both racism – of a naïve and blunt kind they may be unused to – and some isolation in terms of common interests and experiences, religious community, dietary, hair care and other provision. As regards the curriculum, I have anecdotal evidence that having compared mixed and mostly white institutions at close quarters, some BME applicants feel that race will be dealt with more appropriately, more confidently and more comfortably for them among the more diverse population. Unless a course is particularly specialised, it is not surprising that such students gravitate towards the bigger cosmopolitan cites if given a choice.

This is one reason why most black and minority ethnic students are clustered in very few HEIs, mainly new universities in London and to a lesser extent in other big cities. There are seven universities where over 50 per cent of the student body is made up of BME students, and a further five where the percentage is over 40 per cent. Most of them are in London and between them they recruit more BME students than all other HEIs put together. Forty five per cent of British BME people live in London, so this concentration is to be expected.

Local pools of BME students

If the factors described above explain why students are unlikely to leave the areas they know for courses in the 'white highlands', surely HEIs in such areas ought to engage in aggressive outreach to the people who do live nearby? This is the ethnic makeup of secondary schools in the LEAs surrounding five HEIs in one locality in the south of England:

					PERCENTAGES	
	LEA A	LEA B	LEA C	LEA D	LEA E	LEA F
Unclassified	21	13	2	10	4	0.1
White British	82	82.2	85.5	83.1	92.4	87.3
White other	1.5	1.9	4	1.2	1.3	2.5
Mixed white/ Caribbean	0.3	0.3	0.5	0.3	0.2	1
Mixed white/ African	0.2	0.2	0.6	0.2	0.1	0.3
Mixed white/ Asian	0.5	0.3	0.9	0.2	0.2	0.7
Other mixed	0.3	0.5	2	0.4	0.4	0.8
Indian	2	0.2	0.4	0.5	0.3	2.9
Pakistani	1.5	0	0.1	0.1	0.1	1.2
Bangladeshi	0.2	0.2	0.5	1.7	0.2	0.7
Other Asian	0.4	0.2	0.5	0.3	0.1	0.5
Caribbean	0.2	0	0.1	0	0.1	0.5
African	0.4	0.2	1.7	0.3	0.1	0.4
Other black	0	0.1	0.2	0	0.1	0.3
Chinese	0.3	0.3	0.4	0.5	0.3	0.4
Other non-white	0.2	0.4	0.7	0.3	0.2	0.4

SOURCES: MULTIVERSE AND ONS: 2004

(LEAs A and B were clearly unused to ethnic monitoring at the time these figures were gathered, which explains the high number of 'unclassified'.)

These figures were analysed to try to establish the numbers of potential HE entrants in the surrounding postcodes, roughly a 40-mile radius. The percentages were converted into numbers, then divided by five to give the approximate numbers in year 11 (this inflates the figure slightly as some schools have 6th forms). These totals were then reduced according to success rates at GCSE at 16, since this in the short term acts as a gateway to potential HE entry. The following table shows the result of this calculation for some groups. 'Mixed' groups are omitted because of their great diversity and the consequent hazards of extrapolating from national achievement trends to a small local population:

Ethnic group	16 year olds in 40 mile radius (numbers)	% gaining 5+ GCSEs A-C	Potential 'market' (numbers)
Indian	168	65%	109
Pakistani	81	41%	33
Bangladeshi	54	45%	24
Caribbean	26	33%	9
African	559	41%	228
Chinese	108	74%	80

SOURCE: LOCAL LEA PLASC RETURNS

These figures are strikingly low. If every one of these local students came to even the smallest HEI in the region the percentage of BME students would approach 10 per cent. In reality, however, of the 109 local Indian potential HE entrants, perhaps fifteen are likely to be interested in the subjects it offers, subjects which are offered at virtually every HEI in the country.

A tentative conclusion and asking different questions

Reliance on local students severely limits the capacity of HEIs in mainly white areas to recruit more from BME groups. This is due mostly to the low numbers attending local schools and present in the area as mature residents, but is compounded by the magnet effect of the cultural and ethnic feel of more cosmopolitan institutions. When this is combined with the relative status of the institution and the course mix on offer, the obstacles multiply.

The problem could be reformulated. Since most BME groups are not underrepresented in HE as a whole, the issue becomes 'what is it about HEIs in mainly white areas that may attract or repel BME applicants?' 'How can these HEIs attract BME students away from the institutions they currently opt for?'

One answer may be 'why bother?' to which there are two possible replies.

■ The atmosphere and ambiance irrespective of race and culture, especially if the institution is small, might be a positive attraction to some BME students just as it is to some white ones. Some HEIs try to give signals that they offer a small, unintimidating, supportive HEI experience, in a more appealing area to some than a vibrant big city. We do not know if BME applicants are looking for or reading these signals in the same way.

■ It is still an obligation to consider the experience of the majority white students, just as it is in schools. Examining what may be unattractive to BME students can reveal something of the covert and taken for granted racism that may exist in the curriculum and in routine interactions.

In terms of becoming more attractive, there is no magic bullet. Without a critical mass of BME students there is a chicken and egg problem in many HEIs: new applicants will inevitably realise they will be part of a tiny minority. Radically changing the subjects on offer is not a solution: closing whole courses and opening new ones is not practicable. Similarly, even if they are highly aware of an unwelcoming racial ambiance in their local areas, white HEIs can do little about this directly. They cannot alter an inhospitable or hostile climate in the locality, and they cannot provide easy access to a mosque or gurudwara if none exists for 25 miles. In these circumstances, comparatively little can be done to attract students away from where they are currently choosing to go.

Answers?

The reformulation I would stress more, however, mirrors my general argument about schools: even if they are in a white area they cannot say 'no problem here'. Similarly, HEIs who are unable to recruit more BME staff and students, cannot wash their hands of race. And by law they should ensure there are no institutional barriers to recruiting greater numbers of BME staff and students.

Even if HEIs cannot create easy access to an existing faith community if there is not one for miles, they can make clear that provision for independent worship is available. They can also make it known that there is a well-publicised and unambiguous policy supporting BME students in the event of discriminatory experiences, and that this includes curriculum content.

But trying to raise BME overall student numbers in mainly white HEIs should not be the primary focus and emphasis of planning. The Commission for Racial Equality's guide to schools says 'Positive action plans are only meant to be a temporary solution and you must review them regularly. You should not use them if the under-representation, or the particular need, no longer exists'. There are subtler challenges involved in considering the curriculum experienced by all students, and considering the general experience of race equality of everyone in the institution.

Policy should therefore address these challenges. This requires seven related actions, only the first two of which are specifically concerned with BME recruitment:

- Highly targeted student recruiting outreach, concentrating upon subjects known to attract BME students rather than blanket targets

- Short listing all qualified BME applicants for support and academic posts[3]

- Detailed research into the perceptions of current BME students of the institution as a place to study and the locality as a place to live

- A programme of staff training focusing upon case studies and scenarios, to develop awareness and dialogue about curriculum choice, expressions of racism, cultural sensitivity, freedom of speech, language support

- Action plans in each subject area to develop what majority students learn about race equality through their curriculum

- A continuous programme of renewing student awareness in collaboration with the Students' Union

- More recruitment of overseas students, not to placate the CRE and HEFCE but to change the atmosphere and climate. However, it would be ethical to do this only if the previous items are agreed and demonstrably happening.

Strictures about recruitment targets, consultation and impact assessment run the risk of being mechanistic imports that do not travel well. Londocentrism won't work. Change in white areas has to happen without the marked presence of black and minority ethnic people. That is its particular challenge.

Notes

1 In general, post-1992 institutions have higher BME recruitment rates, except for Chinese and Indian students who were more likely to apply for and get into more prestigious institutions (Modood and Ackland, 1998) and do so still, as the Home Office report of 2005 shows.

2 The reasons for this are twofold: the cultural prestige and value of having a large family common in rural areas worldwide persists for some time after populations have migrated, and Bangladeshis are newer migrants than most. The second reason is masked in the aggregated figures for the 16-64 age range: more of the minority groups are at the younger end of the range and hence of childbearing age.

3 All the issues raised in relation to students have some relevance to staff recruitment. Support staff applicants will come overwhelmingly from the locality, but teaching staff recruitment is in principle national. At the same time, the same patterns and choices made by BME students are likely to have been made in the past by people now qualified to teach them they are likely to be concentrated in certain subjects. This is not to discount strategies such as short-listing every BME applicant who meets the criteria, but it should be no surprise if the levels of applications differ in some subject areas.

8

Octopus and Axe: some final notes

In *No Problem Here* I wrote

■ The majority of pupils, it would seem all over Britain, have considerable confusion and misunderstanding about race. Many have high levels of prejudice and hostility

■ This is related not to 'ignorance' but to learned misinformation

■ When faced with racial hostility people often say the answer, and a better future, lies in education

■ Multicultural education as it has been understood may well leave these attitudes untouched

■ No-one will ever challenge these states of minds in pupils unless schools do

■ If we do not take this on then more generations of young people will leave school ill-equipped to critically engage with race

■ If the issue is not tackled in the shires nothing will improve in the cities. (1987: 17)

When I was writing *Still No Problem Here* in 1994 I was fairly gloomy about the dominant climate and the backwards direction in which race equality was going. I have tried to show some optimism in this book, and certainly there are many more positive signs than there were. But the points above still largely apply today, though they apply less.

Making changes is like wrestling with an octopus: there are many tentacles that represent different aspects of the problem, and one cannot always be sure which one is gripping at the time. It's not an octopus though, it's an excusopus; it represents the range of excuses that are invoked for 'things staying as they are'. Institutional racism is defined in Chapter 2 but this is the living embodiment of it; this how institutional racism can work to prevent change.

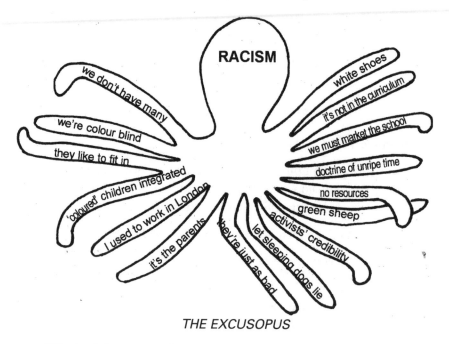

RACISM

We don't have many

we're colour blind

they like to fit in

'coloured' children integrated

I used to work in London

it's the parents

they're just as bad

let sleeping dogs lie

activists' credibility

green sheep

no resources

doctrine of unripe time

we must market the school

it's not in the curriculum

white shoes

THE EXCUSOPUS

'We don't have many'

This is irrelevant in principle but in practice it would be naïve to deny that the presence of actual children can act as a catalyst for action. We saw in Chapter 1 and Chapter 5 how the lives of isolated minority pupils may be blighted by negative treatment they receive on the basis of their colour or culture, and how schools could be sensitive to this. In Chapter 3 I suggested that a challenging starting point for a school policy is to ask how race equality should be addressed when there are no minority children in the school at all, so the emphasis is on what the white children are learning to prepare them for the rest of their lives. This involves what they are learning in a specific way about black and minority ethnic cultures in Britain, what they are learning about racism and discrimination as aspects of social justice, and what they are learning about guarding against stereotyping and prejudice and about themselves and their own actions.

'We're colour blind/ noticing race is racist/ we treat them all the same/ children are just children to me'.

These were discussed in Chapter 1. The first statement is seldom really true but although it entirely fails to grasp the issue it may signal good intent. Noticing race is not racist because to do so recognises that race has effects on people's lives. Indeed not noticing it obscures this and may appear to deny it. Indeed it is racist *not* to notice race when it may be relevant, such as in cases of name-calling (Chapter 5) or in monitoring (Chapter 3). I understand the notion that one may not want to pay attention to someone's colour, that one may simply want to treat and regard him or her as a person, but both are possible. Noticing does not mean treating worse – or treating differently. Discriminating between is not the same as discriminating against.

The assertion of colour blindness is often related to an understandable wish to deny any racism in oneself. Race is something that, for whatever reason, generates a nervous climate. While sexist jokes can be told with impunity and fatuous comments made about female inferiority evoke indulgent smiles, few people in professional circles will admit to being racist, hence the familiar phrase 'I'm not racist but...'. Common perceptions about race and immigration were discussed in Chapter 3, but I may not have stressed enough the courage needed to face this nervousness. It is almost impossible to grow up in Britain without imbibing racist ideas and perceptions and new variations are always prone to slip in unawares. This needs accepting rather than denying. Although there is a bland professional assumption that no teachers would do harm in this area, actually they could, whether by their complacency, nervousness, cowardice, unwillingness to examine their own attitudes, laziness or failure to problematise the issue. The comparison with sexism can be instructive: if I said I had thought as a man about sexism and was completely free of it, I know that few women would believe me, yet people keep making such claims about racism. It's not really convincing to say 'I went on training about this a while ago so I'm okay' because this is like saying 'I had a shower last year and I don't need another one'. 'I'm not racist because my best friend at college was black' is like saying I can't be a sexist because my mother was a woman'.

'I think they like to fit in'

I am interpreting this particularly with regard to culture and ethnicity, rather than race (see Chapters 1 and 4). It is an area that can tax anyone's sensitivity and reflection. This stance may be a variety of the one above, born out of an anxiety about drawing attention to a difference that attracts discrimination. It can also be laziness, since if one satisfies oneself that a child wants to fit in and have no attention paid to their ethnic background there is no need to reflect their presence in the curriculum or perhaps even learn to pronounce their name. But it can also be indicative of the genuine dilemmas that minority pupils and their parents find themselves in, as the quotations from Cline *et al* and from my own work illustrated (Chapter 1). Of course children like to fit in and dread being identified with a stigmatised 'difference', but it is part of a teacher's job to coax out the aspects of someone's identity that are significant to them and enable them to express it. If a white Anglo-Saxon pupil was known to have something interesting and unusual about them, like fluency in Chinese, but was wary of drawing attention to themselves, most teachers would find a way of making it safe to do so and validate it in the process.

'Our 'coloured' children are well integrated'

The misguided use of the word 'coloured' is explored in Chapter 4. The claim may be true in that there is really no name-calling; they may have a good circle of friends and do well in lessons. The potentially misleading thing about such a situation is that we are all, children and adults, perfectly capable of 'exceptionalism': 'you're all right, but it's all the others'; 'I like you 'cos you're like one of us'; 'You're different from the others'. Acceptance of an individual does not necessarily mean that negative stereotypes of that person's group or of different ethnic groups do not prevail. Individual one to one acceptance is no guarantee that broader racist ideas and attitudes are not present.

'I used to work in London so....'

This can be invoked to claim the role of expert – even if the work was brief and many years ago – and can be varied: 'Of course I grew up in

Leicester so...'. Experts can pronounce on different things to different effects (see the next tentacle and 'colour blindness') but either can excuse inaction.

'They're just as bad'/'Racism works both ways...'

When citing the evidence of white hostility to minorities I am often asked 'but have you asked the same question of Black people? Don't they think the same about us?' The question is sometimes asked by an 'expert' with experience elsewhere. There are two answers.

The first is this: if our focus is addressing race equality in white schools it doesn't matter what Pakistanis in Bradford think of white people. It may be interesting but it is not our immediate professional concern and wanting to discuss it signals an exit strategy from a much more uncomfortable discussion. Indian Hindu prejudice towards Muslims, or Caribbean prejudice towards Africans is just another smoke screen.

The second answer involves relative power and relates to white and black pride, as discussed in Chapter 1. It shows wilful disregard of the facts of racial and ethnic disadvantage to say that the feelings of some minorities towards the majority population have either the same psychological basis or the same effects as the racist frame of reference of many whites.

'We must market the school'

Headteachers in white areas have told me that while they agree the issue is important they dare not signal race as high profile in case the school gets a radical image and parents choose a school elsewhere. In peripheral or adjacent areas where minority pupils could potentially apply there could be some interesting dynamics: by having an overt stance on racism who would a school attract – and repel? Defensive comments of this kind should steadily decline now that the law requires all schools to have an unambiguous policy that 'takes proactive steps to tackle racial discrimination, promotes equality of opportunity and promotes good race relations' (see Chapter 3). It should no longer be possible to hide behind this excuse, nor should it be possible for any parent to choose a school on this basis.

'It's the parents'

Aspects of this argument are covered in Chapter 5. Racist ideas may well originate with and be supported by parents, making it hugely difficult for schools to deal with. Home-School partnership agreements, unambiguous statements and guidelines about racist bullying, and publicised race equality policies can signal the school's position to parents, but it will not stop parents mouthing racist sentiments. On the other hand, as I argued in Chapter 5, no school would allow pupils of any age to use certain swear words on the basis that they heard them at home, nor hesitate to tell parents how they felt about obscenities brought from home infecting school vocabulary. Similarly, any parent who tells their offspring to use violence to resolve difficulties at school is always told that the school takes a different view, which it is prepared to enforce by exclusion if necessary. This is not a matter of someone's right to be free to say what they like, it is a matter of other's rights to be free from certain things.

Green sheep

Fortunately there are fewer sightings of these strange beasts than there used to be. The mythical stories about 'PC' or 'loony left' councils 'banning' Baa black sheep because it was allegedly 'racist' have been explored in Chapter 4.

'Let sleeping dogs lie, let's have no controversy'

This is partly a straightforward expression of denial that anything much is amiss and partly a wish to bury it anyway. The evidence this book has provided demonstrates that there is certainly a dog. And the law as outlined in Chapter 3 says it's not supposed to be left to lie around.

Activist's credibility

A favourite way of reducing the legitimacy of enhanced racial equality measures is to undermine the credibility of any advocate, either by reference to their own ethnicity – 'chip on the shoulder'/'special pleading' – or their age, or their inexperience, or their association with other 'liberal' issues – 'it's not a just cause it's just another cause'. Such undermining strategies will always be tried, but in the current climate one's efforts have formal legitimacy thanks to legal requirements, LEA policies, and teacher union documents.

No resources
This is dramatically less true than it was. The internet provides some resources in itself, but more importantly it gives ready access to guidelines, materials and good practice in dozens of LEAs and schools, as well as excellent bookshops and suppliers with good on-line catalogues. See Chapter 6.

The doctrine of the unripe time
This doctrine states 'I agree this is a really important issue, but we'll deal with it next year'. It can sometimes be that a school has so many pressing and urgent concerns that it cannot take on something that requires a good deal of staff reflection. In the pressured and demanding world of schools race equality has to fight for space and recognition, especially in white schools. This book should provide some ammunition for the fight.

'This is not in the curriculum'/'I'm just a subject teacher'
There are specific mentions of race and diversity in formal curriculum documents, but the main curriculum driver is the law, backed up by some of the guidance cited in Chapter 6. One metaphorical vision of the curriculum was suggested in Chapter 6; another is that the curriculum should offer both roots and wings. This has implications beyond race equality, but it's an engaging idea.

White shoes
I was once talking to a group of Bangladeshis about what I was doing for their language in my college. When I had finished someone said 'You people, you don't wear the shoes of racism every day, you don't know where they pinch and where they hurt. We do, but you don't ask us about them, you just keep on designing new shoes, but they're white shoes and they don't fit'. This final tentacle is therefore about consultation, even though consultation is not always easy in a white area.

I argued in Chapter 1 that race equality involves antiracism, and that this is more than celebrating different cultures. The excusopus will not go away if you offer it a samosa or play it steel band music; the tentacles need chopping off.

The most powerful part of the blade to use on the excusopus is *legitimacy*. Working in a national and/or local climate which denied the

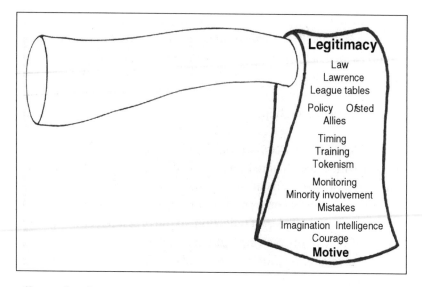

effects of racism, or even its existence, was the miserable situation in the late 1980s and much of the 1990s (see the diagram on page 37 in Chapter 2). I hold no brief for the current government nor do I think its hands are clean with regard to racism, but raising the issue of race equality in white areas is now recognised as much more legitimate than was the case a few years ago. The law requires attention be paid to it, Ofsted is obliged to ask questions about it, league table results may depend upon it, governors have legal duties about it, all schools and LEAs have to have policies on it, the Teacher Training Agency funds its curriculum development. There has been a mushrooming of CPD courses, conferences and publications that target white areas in particular.

Part of the legitimacy can mean new *allies*: in three shire counties the police have driven the monitoring of racist incidents more enthusiastically than some schools. Local community safety partnerships also have a legitimised interest in what pupils learn at school.

The root of this legitimacy is the inquiry into the investigation of Stephen Lawrence's murder. The inquiry showed the investigation to be scandalously and fatally flawed because no one cared enough about a black boy's death. It led the Home Secretary at the time to say:

> We would all be deluding ourselves if we believe that the issues thrown up by this inquiry reflect only upon the police... the inquiry process has revealed some fundamental truths about the nature of our society. (Hansard, 24.02.1999)

The inquiry led directly to the Race Relations Amendment Act.

After legitimacy, there are the three Ts. *Timing* is about tactical campaigning, a programme of action spread over several months, not rushing everything too quickly, not burning out, not forgetting that even when you know your colleagues are wrong no one changes overnight. *Training* is discussed in Chapters 3 and 5.

Tokenism is not to be underestimated nor automatically condemned. All journeys start with the first step and I suspect too many people don't take the first step because they fear the charge of tokenism. I do not think an assembly about a non-Christian festival or a welcome poster in many languages or a reading from a black poet, will in themselves do much to address racism, but they are only tokenist if you think you have done all you need to.

Of the three Ms, *monitoring* has been addressed in Chapters 1 and 3 and touched upon elsewhere. It involves growing confidence in negotiating the sometimes unfamiliar territory of ethnic and racial boundaries, but also a willingness to notice, consider and monitor racist incidents. *Minority involvement* means not making more white shoes, but it is not straightforward (see Chapter 3). An overly metropolitan perspective often speaks of 'communities' but in many white areas there are none. In white areas there are not enough black and minority ethnic people to be a community. There is no easy resolution. Awareness of research evidence of the kind cited here is some help (e.g. Cline *et al*, 2002; de Lima, 2001; Gaine and Lamley, 2003). So is the sensitive engagement of whatever minorities a school may have, and the tapping of any sources and contacts available to the police, social services departments, and the health service – even though in white areas the same people get tired of being the ones asked for help from every agency, especially when it is assumed they will give their time free out of goodwill.

Mistakes, imagination, intelligence and *courage* go together. No one has a blueprint of how to get things right every time; everyone who has been involved in antiracist work has made mistakes that make them cringe when they unwillingly remember them, whether it was being patronising, designing white shoes, drawing attention to someone who preferred not to be noticed, handling incidents insensitively, doing a lesson that replicated stereotypes, alienating racist pupils who needed engaging... But we need the courage to make mistakes and the imagination and intelligence to learn from them.

Motive takes us back to Chapter 1, and the two principled motives. The pragmatic motive is useful and helpful, but will never be enough to bring about real change. The first principled motive is to equip all young people with an appropriate education, to free them from the shackles of uncritical acceptance of racist myths and enable them to relate to people and groups positively and not fearfully or resentfully. The second is to provide a safe and affirming educational experience for minority pupils, born probably from the full engagement Carroll (2003) speaks of. Both of these are moral and educational motives and both have profound long-term positive consequences for British society.

References

The Resources chapter contains additional materials not mentioned elsewhere in the text.

Akhtar, S., and Stronach, I. (1986) 'They call me blacky' – a story of everyday racism in primary schools *Times Educational Supplement*, p 23. 19 September 1986

Bagley, C. A. (1992) Inservice provision and teacher resistance to whole school change in D. Gill, B. Mayor and M. Blair (eds.) *Racism and Education: Structures and Strategies* London: Sage

Ball, S. (1987) *The Micropolitics of the School* London: Routledge

Ball, S. (1994) *Education Reform* Buckingham: Open University Press

Banton, M. (1967) *Race Relations* London: Tavistock

Banton, M. (1987) The Battle of the Name *New Community*, Autumn 1987

Bhavnani, R. (2001) *Rethinking Interventions in Racism* Stoke on Trent: Trentham Books

British Broadcasting Corporation (2002) http://news.bbc.co.uk/hi/english/static/in_depth/uk/2002/race/default.stm

Cameron, D. (1995) *Verbal Hygiene* London: Routledge

Campbell, D. (2002) On PC *Guardian* 25 November 2002

Carroll, P. (2003) Race and Citizenship after 2000: Educational Policy and Practice University of Southampton: Unpublished PhD thesis

Cashmore, E. (1987) *The Logic of Racism* London: Allen and Unwin

Cline, T., Guida de Abreu, G., Fihosy, C., Gray, H., Lambert, H. and Neale, J. (2002) *Minority Ethnic Pupils in Mainly White Schools* London: Department of Education and Skills

Cole, M. and Stuart, J. (2005) 'Do you ride on elephants' and 'never tell them you're German': the experiences of British Asian and black, and overseas student teachers in South East England *British Education Research Journal* 31(3) June

Collins, S. and Begum, H. (2002) *Hidden Voices: A Study of Wiltshire's Minority Ethnic Residents* Trowbridge: Wiltshire Racial Equality Council

Commission for Racial Equality (1999) *Code of Practice for Schools* London: CRE

Commission for Racial Equality (2000) *Learning for All* London: CRE

Connolly, P. and Keenan, M. (2000) *Racial Attitudes and Prejudice in Northern Ireland* Belfast: Northern Ireland Statistics and Research Agency

Cuban (1988) A fundamental puzzle of school reform *Phi Delta Kappa*, 70(5), pp. 341-44

Dadzie, S. (2000) *Toolkit for Tackling Racism in Schools* Stoke on Trent: Trentham Books

de Lima, P (2001) *Needs not Numbers – an exploration of minority ethnic communities in Scotland* London: Commission for Racial Equality and Community Development Foundation

Department for Education and Science (1985) *Education for All (The Swann Report)* London: HMSO

Department for Education and Skills (2003) *Aiming High: Raising the Achievement of Gypsy Traveller Pupils* London: DfES

Department for Education and Skills (2004) *Aiming High: Understanding the Educational Needs of Minority Ethnic Pupils in Mainly White Schools* London: DfES

Department for Education and Skills (2005) www.standards.dfes.gov.uk/ethnic minorities/raising_achievement/whats_new/terminology/

Development Education Dorset (1998) *A Story to Tell* Bournemouth: DEED

Dhalech, M. (1999) *Challenging Racism in the Rural Idyll* Exeter: National Association of Citizens Advice Bureaux West Region

Dhalech, M. (2000) Rural Racial Equality Work in the South West of England *Multicultural Teaching*, 18(2)

Dobbie, P. (2001) A model boat, a golliwog and a question of guilt *Mail on Sunday* 25 February 2001

Donald, P. Gosling, S. Hamilton, J. (1995) *'No Problem Here?' Children's Attitudes to Race in a Mainly White Area* Glasgow: SCRE

Downing, J. and Husband, C. (2005) *Representing Race* London: Sage

Dunant, S. (Ed) (1994) *The War of the Words: the Political Correctness Debate* London: Virago

Dunn, L. (1975) Race and Biology in L. Kuper (Ed) *Race, Science and Society* Paris: UNESCO

Education Leeds (2004) *Promoting Race Equality in Schools* Leeds: Education Leeds

Elkins, C. (2005) Britain's Gulag: The Brutal End of Empire in Kenya London: Cape

Eysenck, H.J. (1971) *Race, Intelligence and Education* London: Temple Smith

Figueroa, P. (1984) Race Relations and Cultural Differences: Some ideas on a racial frame of reference in G. Verma and C. Bagley (eds) *Race Relations and Cultural Differences* London: Croom Helm

Fryer, P. (1984) *Staying Power: The History of Black People in Britain* London: Pluto

Fullan, M. (1991) *The New Meaning of Educational Change* London: Cassell

Gaine, C. (1987) *No Problem Here* London: Hutchinson

Gaine, C. (1995) *Still No Problem Here* Stoke on Trent: Trentham Books

Gaine, C. (2000) Anti-racist Education in White Areas: the Limits and Possibilities of Change *Race, Ethnicity and Education*, Vol 3 (1) Feb

Gaine, C. (2001a) 'If it's not hurting it's not working': teaching teachers about race *Research Papers in Education* Vol 16 (1) March

Gaine, C. (2001b) Promoting Equality and equal opportunities: school policies in Hill, D and Cole, M. (eds) (2001) *Schooling and Equality* London: Kogan Page

Gaine, C. (2005) Minority Ethnic Experience in Herefordshire Unpublished report commissioned by Herefordshire Council

Gaine, C. and Lamley, K. (2003) *Racism and the Dorset Idyll* Bournemouth: Dorset Race Equality Council

Gaine, C. and Pearce, L. (eds) (1988) *Anti Racist Education in White Areas* Report of NAME Conference Chichester: NAME

Gerwirtz, S. (1997) Can all schools be successful? An exploration of the determinants of school 'success' Paper presented at the British Educational Research Association Annual Conference (September 11-14: University of York)

Gillborn, D. (1995) *Racism and Antiracism in Real Schools* Buckingham: Open University Press

Givens, N. and Bennett, S. (2004) Tentative progress in a Mainly White Setting: hearing from trainee teachers from ethnic minority backgrounds *Race Equality Teaching* 23 (1) Autumn

Gough, H. and Gaine, C. (2002) *Minority Ethnic Experience in the Chichester* District Chichester: UCC

Gould, N. (1995) Curveball in F. Fraser (Ed.) *The Bell Curve Wars* New York: Basic Books

Groom, N. (2000) 'I could probably say it 1,000 ways and they'd probably all offend...' *Times Higher Education Supplement* 9 June

Guardian (2002) Special report: religious affairs *Guardian* June 17

Guardian (2004) Four out of 10 whites do not want black neighbour, poll shows Guardian January 14

Guardian (2004) Newspapers flout ruling on asylum seekers *Guardian* December 31

Hall, L. (1986) Language, Race and Colour, in Frank Palmer (ed), *Anti-Racism, an Assault on Freedom and Value* London: Sherwood Press

Hall, S. (1990) *Race, the Floating Signifier* Northampton, Mass: Media Education Foundation

Hamilton, C., Rejtman-Bennett, R., and Roberts, M. (1999) *Racism and Race Relations in Predominantly White Schools: Preparing pupils for life in a multi-cultural society* Colchester: Children's Legal Centre

Henderson, P. and Kaur, R. (1999) *Rural Racism in the UK* London: Community Development Foundation

Herrnstein, R. and Murray, C. (1994) *The Bell Curve* New York: Free Press

Higher Education Funding Council for England (2005) www.hefce.ac.uk

Home Office (1982) *The Brixton Disorders 1981: Report of an Inquiry by Lord Scarman* London: HMSO

Home Office (2000) *Race Relations Amendment Act* London: Home Office

Home Office Race, Cohesion, Equality and Faith Directorate (2005) *Race Equality in Public Services* London: Home Office

Huberman, M (1983) Recipes for busy kitchens *Knowledge, Creation, Diffusion, Utilization*, 4 478-510

Jay, E. (1992) *Keep Them in Birmingham* London: Commission for Racial Equality

Jeffcoate, R. (1979) *Positive Image: Towards a Multicultural Curriculum* London: Readers and Writers

Kenny, N. (1997) *It Doesn't Happen Here* Taunton: Somerset Racial Equality Network

King, A., and Reiss, M. (eds) (1993) *The Multicultural Dimension of the National Curriculum* London: Falmer

Kirp, D. (1979) *Doing Good by Doing Little* London: University of California Press

Klein. G. (1993) *Education Towards Race Equality* London: Continuum International

Lewis, J (2004) http://womenshistory.about.com/library/weekly/aa010329b.htm

Luthra, M. and Oakley, R. (1991) *Combating Racism Through Training: a review of approaches to race training in organisations* London: Economic and Social Research Council

Lyseight-Jones, P. (1990) A management of Change Perspective: turning the whole school around in Cole, M (ed) *Education for Equality* London, Routledge

Macpherson, W (1999) *The Stephen Lawrence Inquiry: Report of an Inquiry by Sir William Macpherson of Cluny* London: Home Office

Major, C. (1971) *Black Slang: A Dictionary of African American Talk* London: Routledge Kegan Paul

Massey, I. (1991) *More Than Skin Deep* Sevenoaks: Hodder and Stoughton

Milner, D. (1975) *Children and Race* London: Penguin

Milner, D. (1983) *Children and Race: Ten Years On* London: Ward Lock

Modood, T. (1992) *Not Easy Being British* Stoke on Trent: Trentham Books

Modood, T and Acland, T. (eds) (1998) *Race and Higher Education* (PSI Report) London: Policy Studies Institute

Modood, T. and Berthoud, R. with Lakey, J., Nazroo, J., Virdee, S., and Beishon, S. (1997) *Ethnic Minorities in Britain* London: Policy Studies Institute

MORI (2002) www.mori.com/mrr/2002/c020621.shtml

National Association of Head Teachers (2005) *Race Equality and Multi-cultural Education* (Primary Leadership paper 14) Haywards Heath: NAHT

National Council for Voluntary Organisations (1994) *Challenging Rural Racism* London: NCVO

National Union of Schoolmasters Union of Women Teachers (1999) *Education and Race* Birmingham: NASUWT

National Union of Teachers (2001) *Anti-Racist Curriculum Guidelines* London: NUT

National Union of Teachers (2004) *Do Not Tolerate Intolerance* London: NUT

Norfolk Race Equality Council (1994) *Not in Norfolk* Norwich: Norfolk and Norwich REC

Office of National Statistics http://neighbourhood.statistics.gov.uk London: ONS

Office of National Statistics www.statistics.gov.uk London: ONS

Osler, A. and Morrison, M. (2000) *Inspecting Schools for Race Equality: Ofsted's Strengths and Weaknesses, a report for the Commission for Racial Equality* Stoke on Trent: Trentham Books and the CRE

Powney, J., McPake, J., Hall, S. and Lyall, L. (1998) *Education of Minority Ethnic Groups in Scotland: A Review of Research* Glasgow; University of Glasgow (SCRE)

Richardson, R. (2004a) *Islamophobia: issues, challenges and action* Stoke on Trent: Trentham Books and the Uniting Britain Trust

Richardson, R. (2004b) *Here, There and Everywhere* Stoke on Trent: Trentham Books

Rosenhaft, E. (1998) www.h-net.org/~women/threads/disc-braburn.html

Runnymede Trust (1994) *A Very Light Sleeper* London: Runnymede Trust

Runnymede Trust (1997) *Islamophobia: a Challenge for Us All* London: Runnymede Trust

Runnymede Trust (2000) *The Future of Multi-Ethnic Britain* London: Profile Books

Saranson, S. (1990) *The Predictable Failure of School Reform* San Francisco: Jossey-Bass

Sarup, M. (1986) *The Politics of Multiracial Education* London: Routledge Kegan Paul

Sawyers, (1998) Don't mention the N word *Guardian* March 20 p.6

Sheridan, L. (2002) Islamophobia: The new racism? In The Muslim Council for Britain (ed.). *The Quest for Sanity: reflections on September 11 and the aftermath* London: Muslim Council of Britain

Stone, M. (1981) *The Education of the Black Child in Britain* London: Fontana

Tomlinson, S. (1990) *Multicultural Education in White Schools* London: Batsford

Troyna, B. and Hatcher, R. (1992) *Racism in Children's Lives* London: Routledge

Troyna, B. and Williams, J. (1986) *Racism, Education and the State* London: Croom Helm

United Nations High Commissioner for Refugees (UNHCR) (2004) Cited in www.refugee-action.org.uk

Universities and Colleges Admissions Service www.ucas.ac.uk

van den Berghe, P. (1984) Racial Theories in E. Cashmore (ed) *Dictionary of Race and Ethnic Relations* London: Routledge

van Dijk, T. (1987) *Communicating Racism* Newbury Park: Sage

van Dijk, T. (1993) *Elite Discourse and Racism* Newbury Park: Sage

van Driel, B. (2004) *Confronting Islamophobia in Educational Practice* Stoke on Trent: Trentham Books

Williams, P. (1997) *Seeing a Colour Blind Future* London: Virago

Wilson, M. (1987) *Mixed Race Children* London: Allen and Unwin

Index

anti-semitism 102

black 82-9, 92-3
BBC 9, 84
Britkid 125

Census categories 79-80
colour
    blindness 21, 25, 27,
    173
    noticing it 21
    significance of 1, 4,
    10, 14, 22-4, 74, 81,
    84
'coloured' 82-9, 91
Commission for Racial
    Equality 47, 50, 54,
    65, 168,
Conservative Party 10, 30,
    32-3, 35

daily newspapers 8, 9, 13,
    56, 71, 86, 87, 98
Department for
    Education and Skills
    6, 7, 50, 91,
diversity in UK 4, 5, 156

economic inequality and
    race 12-13, 56, 160,
    162
Education Support
    Grants (ESGs) 31, 32
Elliot, Jane *see Eye of the
    Storm*

ethnic monitoring 23, 52-
    4, 79, 81, 157, 179
ethnicity 24, 26, 77-81, 91
    and Asian people
    77-8, 84, 95-6
Eye of the Storm (film) 109

gollywogs 98-9

higher education
    factors in minority
    choices 160-164
    minorities' subject
    choices 161-3
    race equality
    strategy 155, 167-9
    racial ambiance in
    163-4, 167
Higher Education
    Funding Council for
    England 157
Home Office 13, 17, 32,
    56, 158, 160,

immigration 10
Islam *see* Muslims

Labour Party 7, 8, 30, 33,
    34
loony left *see* political
    correctness

Macpherson Report, 34
    definition of racist
    incident 118-9

MORI 8
multicultural
    education 17, 27, 28,
    29, 32
    range of meanings
    3-4, 16
Muslims 9-13, 14, 19, 95,
    104

National Association of
    Head Teachers 48,
national policies 9, 19, 29,
    30-38
National Union of
    Teachers 102
'nigger' 89, 94-5
numbers of minorities 4-5
    in higher education
    156-7 159,

Ofsted *see* school
    inspection

paradox of anti-racism
    21-22

parents 105-7176
political correctness 33,
    85-90
    origin of term 87-8
poverty *see* economic
    inequality and race
public attitudes on race
    7-10

pupils' racial attitudes
    discovering them
    19-20
    for other aspects *see*
    racism

race 70-77
race equality
    and educational
    goals 17, 18, 49
    motives for 18, 63
    higher education
    strategy 155, 167-9
Race Relations
    Amendment Act 7,
    34, 45, 46, 153-5
racism
    and action 19
    between pupils 104-
    8, 113-4
    biological 70-77
    levels of operation
    35-42
    distinction from
    bullying 115
    distinction from
    racialism 113
    examples in
    attitudes and
    experiences 2, 8, 9,
    10, 14, 15-20, 56, 68,
    102, 175
    engagement with 43
    from minorities 175

institutional 26, 39-
40, 172-7
internalised 83
in higher education
environment 163-4,
167
in rural areas 13
in teachers' ideas 25,
28, 56-9
in treatment of
people 15, 103
recognising it 103
surviving it 14, 16, 22
special nature of
108-112
unwillingness to
report 106-8
racist incidents
    distinguishing from
    other name calling
    108-112
    involving staff 123-4
    Macpherson
    definition 118-9
    recording 121-2
    school examples
    104-7, 113
    staff training 116-
    123
    white perceptions
    about 119
refugees 9, 35, 97
religious hatred 12

school inspection 34, 36,
43
school policies 46
    action plan 63-5
    catering for all
    pupils 48
    CRE advice 52-3
    ideal content 46-7
    protecting
    minorities 49
    suggested outline
    54-5
subject choice in higher
    education 161-3
Spike Lee 95
Stephen Lawrence 22, 34,
118, 178
Swann Report 31, 32, 75

teacher attitudes 25, 28,
56-9
tokenism 28, 179
Travellers 7, 44, 48, 98
training typologies 60-63

United Nations High
    Commissioner for
    Refugees (UNHCR) 9
Universities and Colleges
    Admissions Service
    162

white areas definition 6
whiteness 22, 82